THE GREAT
VIRGINIA
FLOOD
OF 1870

PAULA F. GREEN

THE
History
PRESS

Published by The History Press
Charleston, SC
www.historypress.com

Front cover: On October 1, 1870, the photographer C.R. Rees captured the only known photo of the 1870 flood in Richmond, Virginia near where Main Street Station now stands. *Image used with the permission of the Virginia Museum of History and Culture.*

First published 2020

ISBN 9781540243959

Library of Congress Control Number: 2020938461

Dedicated to all those whose lives were affected by the 1870 flood, especially those who were marginalized and whose stories were lost to time.

CONTENTS

ACKNOWLEDGEMENTS

There are so many people who have helped and guided me over the course of writing this book and the thesis it's derived from. I want to first thank my editor Kate Jenkins for supporting this project when I pitched it to her in January and being so patient with me since this is my first book and we were working on a crazy fast deadline to meet publication timelines for September. I feel very lucky to have had her guidance, encouraging words of wisdom and pragmatism when she became aware of the extent to which I'm a perfectionist. On that same note, thank you to Julie Gochenour, whose serendipitous conversation last fall led to an introduction to Kate Jenkins and The History Press. I really appreciate her faith in me.

In terms of research support, especially while the world was fighting a pandemic, I'd like to sincerely thank Tamara Gibson, director of Port Republic Museum, for thoroughly poring through the archives with me on a cold February afternoon before the world went on lockdown; Connie Geary at the Scottsville Museum for answering several questions via email and helping with research for this area; George Best, a friend and park ranger at Harpers Ferry, who patiently answered so many questions about the geography of the area; Mary Laura Kludy, VMI's archives and records management specialist, for her help securing photographs; Meg Hughes, director of collections at the Valentine Museum; Graham Dozier, visual resources manager at Virginia Museum of History & Culture; Laura Hassell, executive director of the White House Farms Foundation; Nancy Karnes, director of the Shenandoah Heritage Center; and Jim Heflin, archivist at the Warren Heritage Society.

ACKNOWLEDGEMENTS

The original thesis required a lot of direction, and I'm very grateful to my thesis committee for their insightful comments and suggestions, which led to the framework for this book. My sincere gratitude goes to Dr. David Dillard, Dr. Evan Friss, Dr. Skip Hyser and Dr. Carole Nash for all their help and guidance over the years. Additionally, for their gracious work with locating primary sources, I would like to extend a thank-you to the staff at the Library of Virginia, Virginia Museum of History and Culture, Valentine Museum, University of Virginia's Special Collections, Warren Heritage Society, Page County Clerk's Office and the Warren County Clerk's Office.

I also need to extend a heartfelt thank-you to my friends and colleagues at the JMU Libraries. I could not ask for a better work group. Thank you to Mikki Butcher, April Beckler and Nicole Sutherland in the Interlibrary Loan Office, who have been so supportive and encouraging; Mark Purington, for helping to scan a fragile antique photograph; Julia Merkel, for reframing and preserving a portrait; Allison Lyttle for surprising me with writing snacks; and so many others, including our wonderful dean, Bethany Nowviskie. I'm truly lucky to be a part of this team!

A special thank-you to my mom, Carolyn Kyger, who graciously helped proof and edit, along with my amazing friends Katie Richie and April Beckler for taking the time to read this and give honest feedback while putting my mind at ease about the direction of this work.

Thank you, Tony Lechmanski, for being an endless well of support and encouragement.

To my friend Annie Layne, who passed away while I was working on this, words can't express how much I miss you, lady. One of the last things she said to me was in reference to this project. After getting sidetracked in a conversation about art, agency, creative boundaries and missing folks during COVID-19, I mentioned something about my deadline, and she said, "Get to weeeeerk!" That phrase rang in my head as I worked on final edits the week she left our realm. The world lost an incredible, unique beacon of light.

Finally, to all my friends and family who exhibited immense patience while I worked on this research, I can't thank you enough. I sincerely appreciate everyone who checked in to make sure I wasn't overdoing it. Thank you: Mom, Dad, Francene, Stephen, Bert, Christian, Thomas, Bill S., Uncle John, Rudy, Aunt Pat, Trish, Liz and Anthony, Chad and Jen, Morgan and Alisha, Tony, Katie, Wes, April, Allison, Nicole, Angel, Ashley, Ivan, Annie, Teagan, Saman and so many others.

My heart is full at having such a wonderful support system. Thank you all! ♥

INTRODUCTION

It was a fearful sight as house after house succumbed to the current and went dashing in the stream amid the fearful shouts of their occupants: while suddenly the extinguishment of light and the floating away of a dark mass of debris told too painfully the story of death.
—New York Times, *October 3, 1870.*[1]

The waves rocked and pushed what was left of the log cabin down the river. From the hills surrounding Harpers Ferry, spectators watched as an elderly African American woman passed the town "sailing down the river on a piece of roof."[2] This fierce lady was calmly smoking a short pipe on the roof of her former home after surviving the flood for nearly seventy miles from somewhere in Page County, Virginia. She traveled by roof another three miles over some intense rapids before being rescued at Weverton, Maryland.[3]

Despite the terrible loss of her home and survival of an incredible journey along a flooded river, the newspapers failed to even print her name. This story is a good example of marginalization that was pervasive in the historic record, especially for African Americans, women and the socioeconomically disadvantaged. The story of the 1870 flood that engulfed parts of Virginia, West Virginia and Maryland cannot be told without addressing the systemic racism, misogyny and discrimination that affected the lens through which all information was relayed and recorded for posterity. This was a devastating event for all who lived along the waterways, but representation was often skewed and biased, often eliminating the names of casualties or downplaying the plight of some people.

At the time, the flood was considered the worst in memory to have affected the area in terms of destruction, casualties and depth of water. Over one hundred people lost their lives, and countless were left homeless and/or without employment. It's important to remember this event, not only because of the lives lost and stories of chaotic destruction but also to learn from these events and understand how people fared when there wasn't access to modern disaster-relief programs or even organized charities like the American Red Cross, which was not yet in existence.

To get a sense of the scale of destruction and how the flood impacted those along its path, the first three chapters are devoted to stories from the affected areas. These sections provide a detailed examination of the storm and resulting flood damage with analysis of the flood's impact or historical context interspersed. Since the National Weather Service was not yet in existence and there are no official records or statistical data for this weather event, these sections also work as a timeline and serve to outline the broad geographic boundaries. Chapter 1 begins with an overview of the storm and starts the geographic trek from Lewis Creek in Staunton, Augusta County, Virginia, to Front Royal in Warren County, Virginia, where the north and south forks of the Shenandoah River converge. Chapter 2 follows the flooding along the main stem of the Shenandoah until it reached Harpers Ferry, wreaking havoc in that location. Here, the Shenandoah meets the Potomac River and the floodwaters turned toward Washington, D.C. Chapter 3 covers the flooding along the James River and its tributaries. Starting in Rockbridge County, the North (now Maury) River washed out everything in its path until merging with the James at Balcony Falls. Here, the meandering waterway's path turns eastward, passing through Lynchburg, Scottsville and eventually reaching Richmond, Virginia. These three chapters attempt to immerse the reader in the flood experience and give a fuller sense of the scale of the damage. By examining the destruction as a whole event rather than a sectional local history, the reader gets a better sense of the immense scale through the stories of the people who were affected. While the chapters touch on the commercial economic loss, the plight of people who lost their homes or lives and telling their stories are the main focus of these sections.

Chapter 4 turns to the subject of relief for the sufferers of the flood. While the majority of aid came from nearby neighbors and residents of the region, there was also a statewide legislative relief fund. Looking at relief further illuminates the scale of property destruction and loss while also shedding light on post–Civil War charity efforts during Reconstruction. The language and appeals of the relief efforts often invoked and utilized healing sentiments between Virginia and certain northern states, specifically New York, Pennsylvania and Maryland. The healing rhetoric expressed a desire to move forward and leave the wounds of the Civil War in the past.

This section also delves into how localized responses in different affected areas were influenced by local politics and regional differences. Additionally, a large section of this analysis is devoted to the statewide relief effort that was initiated by former Confederate general John D. Imboden. His letter to the *New York Herald* is examined for its political undertones and historical context. The ways in which the varying committees approached relief help modern readers to better understand regional relationships. Finally, this part also briefly touches on how the death of General Robert E. Lee less than two weeks after the flood changed the tone of attention from flood relief to mourning and fundraising for memorial statuary. Together, these themes reveal different ways in which the residual effects of the Civil War and Reconstruction influenced philanthropy in the wake of an extensive natural disaster. Finally, chapter 5 takes a brief look at public memory and how references to this flood appear in subtle ways across the region.

Much has changed in Virginia over the past 150 years. Besides taking place five years after the Civil War in the midst of Reconstruction, the populace has increased dramatically. For example, in 1870, the entire population of the state was 1,225,163. By comparison, if you took everyone currently living in Virginia Beach, Norfolk, Chesapeake, Newport News and Hampton and spread them throughout the state, there would still be an additional 24,000 more people. It was also vastly more rural, with 88.1 percent of the population living in nonurban areas. In fact, there were only fifteen cities according to 1870 census data, the largest of which was the city of Richmond, with 51,038 people. This alone makes a difference in terms of relief because it was much harder to see and grasp all of the damage statewide when it was so spread out. Not all rural locations had a media outlet to relay information to the more densely populated areas.

Monetary damage estimates are also difficult to follow because of how the value of the dollar decreased over time. According to one estimate, $1.00 in 1870 would be approximately equivalent to $20.45 today. However, sometimes it's easier to understand the state of inflation through anecdote. In September 1870, Philena Carkin was advanced two months of her teacher's salary and traveling expenses from Boston to Charlottesville. She wrote in her travel journal that she was able to give two ladies a temporary loan of $10.00 because she "had over a hundred dollars on hand" due to her wage advance.[4] It may resonate more to think about $100.00 being two months' salary and travel expenses from a well-paying job. If you were to skim through the Virginia 1870 census, often those who were making ends meet may have had around $100.00 to $500.00 in personal property. Richer folks, like Senator John F. Lewis, who had a large farm and mill in Rockingham County, had a real estate value of $65,000 and personal property worth $3,000. In contrast, the miller for his farm, A.L. Wagner, had $400 in personal property and no real estate value. Knowing their occupations and household wealth may give a sense of the disparity between the very wealthy and the middle class. Unfortunately, it's not so different from the state of things today.

Although this book mainly follows damage along the waterways, it's important to acknowledge how the loss of bridges severed transportation arteries along other routes, including railroad, wagon and pedestrian roads. In some instances, the bridges lost were not rebuilt for years, often being replaced by ferries until enough funds were raised by the community or bridge company. In Page County, residents went without the bridge at White House for forty years before a replacement was reconstructed. Although unconnected to the flood, Hatton Ferry in Scottsville began operation in the 1870s, and it is the last pole-operated ferry in the United States. It is generally in operation on the weekends from April to October. Its living history provides a good example of how communities without access to a bridge were dependent on water levels, skilled labor and weather conditions for travel.

Unfortunately, and unsurprising for the time, the marginalization of minorities, women and those with a lower socioeconomic status is commonplace and pervasive. So often the names of flood victims fitting into these categories are missing from the historic record. When mentioned, African Americans are rarely recorded by full name, unless they were well known in their community or had achieved a higher level of wealth. The average person is referred to by his or her employment, gender and age, such as "the old ferryman and his wife" in Fluvanna County or "Mrs. Ransom's servant girl" in Lynchburg. When possible, the clues about their lives have led to identification and the restoration of their identities in this story. Women are often referred to in relation to their husbands or fathers. For example, Louisa Boude, who was married to the Reverend Adam Poe Boude, was elusive. She's called Mrs. A.P. Boude in newspaper records, and that family was initially missing from the 1870 census. It took a lot of digging through other census years and records to find Louisa's first name and her son Rudolph. Trying to locate identities through the lens of what wealthy white men writing the narrative thought was important was often difficult but an important element of the story.

While this book attempts to include as many diverse voices and perspectives as possible, source limitations ultimately restrict a fuller understanding of the flood from a variety of firsthand perspectives. The most common and well-documented interpretation of the flood comes from middle-to-upper-class white males. Occasionally, letters and other sources representing white female and lower-middle-class individuals have been located. However, firsthand accounts from African American sources or those living with limited means prior to the flood were unable to be located. This is part of a systemic problem where marginalizing minority, female and the socioeconomically depressed was, and often still is, commonplace. In this instance, those perspectives were overlooked in the original media and archival collecting practices. As such, the scholarship relating to this event does not encompass all viewpoints from a firsthand perspective. Despite the limitations, every effort has been made to represent and discuss diverse groups through available source materials in order to tell a more complete story of those who were affected by the freshet.[5]

Reports of the Great Virginia Flood can be found in the majority of American newspapers following the disaster. Papers from Baltimore to San Francisco contain coverage in varying degrees. Most recount the damage that occurred in better-known industrial or urban areas, such as Richmond, Lynchburg and Harpers Ferry. However, areas closer to the region or with significant business interests there had a tendency to cover the event in incredible detail. For example, the *New York Times* ran at least twelve articles relating to the flood between October 1 and 6, 1870, with several spanning multiple columns. The extensive *New York Times* coverage is likely related to business relationships between New York and Virginia companies and the paper's large readership, which may have been interested in the topic. Additionally, *Harper's Weekly* and *Frank Leslie's Illustrated Newspaper*, both weekly illustrated papers with a large national circulation, covered the event with written information and several engravings. The extent of newspaper coverage indicates that the event was of great interest to the American public at the time of its occurrence.

Newspaper coverage was the primary source of mass communication and media coverage about the flood and its aftermath. As a source, it is invaluable for opening a window into the past that reveals local culture and immediate reactions to certain events. However, its consistent reliability is debatable. On one hand, newspapers were often utilized as mechanisms for disseminating public notices and keeping official committee records. For example, the minute book of the Richmond Chamber of Commerce in 1870 often features cut-out newspaper articles as official minutes instead of handwritten notes.[6] This indicates the news' perceived reliability; however, there are times where the inaccuracies are glaring. Local hearsay in the wake of the flood often erroneously pronounced people dead. As a result, it is not uncommon to see stories retracted several days later. Additionally, it is important to acknowledge political bias and varying personal agendas, such as embellishing a story to be paid a higher wage for column length.

To avoid potential inaccuracies, individual newspaper accounts of damage and death have been compared to competing newspaper articles and a variety of other available source materials. By consulting personal papers, census records, diaries, ledgers and other miscellaneous records, source materials were cross-checked for accuracy when possible. The variety of sources fleshed out the event from multiple perspectives and helped to confirm specific events, deaths and instances of damage. The result is a more comprehensive, but still incomplete, interpretation of the flood and its aftermath.

Primary sources were located in Special Collections at the University of Virginia, the Library of Virginia, the Valentine Museum, the Virginia Museum of History and Culture, the Port Republic Museum, Scottsville Museum, the Virginia Military Institute Archives, census records and various local court records. The secondary works that discuss the flood most often reduce it to a county or city level. Books such as *Scottsville on the James* by Virginia Moore, *A Short History of Page County, Virginia* by Harry M Strickler, *The Strange Story of Harper's Ferry* by Joseph Barry and *Lynchburg and Its People* by W. Asbury Christian discuss the local aspects of the flood. However, these works most often restate local newspaper coverage and recount community memories in the space of a chapter or less. Unfortunately, there are no secondary sources that focus on the 1870 flood or attempt to cover it as a regional event.

In order to better understand the flood in terms of its historical context, several secondary works have been invaluable for examining both Reconstruction in Virginia and contemporary nineteenth-century disaster responses. Richard Lowe's *Republicans and Reconstruction in Virginia, 1856–70* provides an in-depth account of Virginia's changing political climate from the prewar years to Virginia's readmission to the Union. *Yankee Town, Southern City* by Steven Elliott Tripp delves into the dynamics of Lynchburg City during this era by exploring race relations, socioeconomic differences, local politics and the role of religion. This book does an excellent job of analyzing the city's changing relationship with caring for the poor and is particularly helpful for unpacking the nuances of Lynchburg's flood relief efforts.

With regards to sources that examine other contemporaneous disasters, Elizabeth Sharpe's *In the Shadow of the Dam: The Aftermath of the Mill River Flood of 1874* provides a good comparison of how several communities dealt with a devastating flood that occurred unexpectedly when a dam broke. The flood is smaller in terms of the geographical impact but was absolutely devastating to the communities along the Mill River in Massachusetts. Sharpe thoroughly examines the flood responses in each community and how local politics played a role in the recovery efforts. This scholarship provides an excellent comparison for how relief funds were raised, thought about and distributed during the early 1870s. While not as close of a comparison, Karen Sawislak's analysis of the Chicago Fire relief efforts in her book *Smoldering City: Chicagoans and the Great Fire, 1871–1874* devotes an entire chapter to aid analysis and how relief was provided on a large scale. Her examination into politics of relief illuminated the use of social stratification and efforts to control the urban poor. While the Great Chicago Fire was a different type of disaster in terms of location, scale and publicity, it is helpful to look at Sawislak's work as an additional source of relief thought, especially since the fire occurred almost exactly one year after the 1870 flood.

Although this is a tale that's become obscured over time, its rippling effects became part of the story of this region. By changing the location of towns, causing deaths of entire families, wiping out certain businesses and altering the way we traveled, it affected the trajectory of the region. For those who lived through it, the flood was regarded as one of the worst events in the history of the area, prompting one commentator to proclaim it was "a scene of ruin and desolation scarcely paralleled by the havoc effected during the late war."[7]

THE WINDING FORKS OF THE SHENANDOAH

Staunton to Warren County, Virginia

To the ear it sounded as if the elements were holding a concert on the grandest scale of musical combinations. The pattering and silvery tinkle of the millions of rain-drops—the trickling and murmur of thousands of rills—the babbling and splashing of the streams—the roar of the innumerable cataracts, and the sullen, deep, and subdued sounds of the mighty flood and the breaking waves all united in a chorus, that can neither be described nor conceived of in its solemn grandeur.
—Virginia Gazette, *October 7, 1870*

In the darkness, the bell tolled a slow, moribund ring as the waves of the flood rocked a building recently lifted from its foundation in the Shenandoah Iron Works. Around 9:00 p.m., among the dizzying noise of rushing water and crashing buildings, the bell of the carpenter's shop sounded its last ring when the entire structure was swept away and carried down the Shenandoah River. Mr. Stalling, a German painter who was visiting the ironworks, dramatically summed up the scene by exclaiming, "Mein Gott! It sounded like the death knell of the world!"[8] Similar stories and accounts of unexpected terror engulfed the news and grabbed the American public's attention after the flood swept a wave of unprecedented death and devastation over a large region encompassing parts of Virginia, West Virginia and Maryland.[9]

THE STORM CONDITIONS FOR A DISASTER

A sprinkle of rain began to soak into the dry, cracked earth on the afternoon of Wednesday, September 28, 1870.[10] At the start of the storm, those living in the western part of Virginia were overjoyed that an extended drought appeared to be over. According to one newspaper, the drought in Richmond caused gardens to be "burnt up" to the point that fall vegetables almost completely disappeared from local markets.[11] Many local papers in the storm's radius contained either excitement or relief at the prospect of rain. The *Charlottesville Chronicle* commented that "some rain fell here on Wednesday after an unprecedented drought. The dust in some parts of the town was four inches deep."[12] Over fifty miles away, in Page County, the *Shenandoah Valley* reported that "by nightfall the whole Page valley were [*sic*] rejoicing over the grateful cessation of the long and severe drought that had parched and baked and burned their fertile fields."[13] The day before the storm, the drought was referenced in the *Staunton Spectator*'s witty humor column, which detailed a specific way that a New Hampshire preacher prayed for rain: "Not a tearin, drivin rain, such as harrers up the face of natur, but a drizzling, sozzlin' rain, such as lasts all day and pretty much all night."[14] The quoted prayer echoed the sentiments of many Virginia residents who hoped for a good soaking rain to ameliorate the drought-stricken land.

The lengthy nature of the drought pushed the prospect of rain to the forefront of public thought since it affected everyday life for most people in the region. Those who made a living through agriculture depended on rain for their crops and livelihoods. From an industrial perspective, mills, iron furnaces and other industries were dependent on, and typically powered by, river and stream water. Additionally, shipping and transportation along the inland waterways and canals depended on sufficient water levels for boats to move efficiently. Finally, water provided the most basic necessity for all living beings as a part of their daily sustenance. Without an adequate water supply, the consequences could have been dire, immediate and long-lasting for the entire region, through basic necessity and a variety of economic consequences.

Unfortunately, excitement at the prospect of rain became short-lived when the storm changed from a steady rain to a heavy downpour over the course of Wednesday night and Thursday morning. The earliest mention of the storm begins in Charlottesville, where "a steady rain set in this vicinity" around noon on Wednesday, September 28.[15] From there, the storm appears to have moved west, drenching Lexington in the afternoon and moving north through the Shenandoah Valley. In Rockbridge County, John Horn noted in his sawmill ledger that the rain began "at 1 o'clock [and] never stopt [*sic*] until the 30th at 12 o'clock."[16] Another account stated that "rain began to fall in the upper part of Page County, about 5 o'clock on the afternoon of Wednesday, the 28th, from a black and heavy rain cloud, which made its appearance from the south-east."[17] While the origin of the storm is unclear, contemporary accounts indicate that it was a massive storm that hung over the region from Wednesday through Friday.

As Mr. Stalling called "Mein Gott!" while the bell tolled in the Shenandoah Iron Works in Page County, the storm had already caused flooding across the region. However, the worst of it would occur over the next eighteen hours. Regional accounts show consistent similarities to the timing and duration of the rain; the downpour converted the waterways in its path into sweeping torrents. The normally peaceful veins of water became cutting scythes of unstoppable power as the rain brought death, destruction and economic loss to families and communities that were in the path of the rushing water.

STAUNTON AND AUGUSTA COUNTY, VIRGINIA

The rain commenced near Staunton in the afternoon of Wednesday, September 28, and continued "almost incessantly, from that time till Friday."[18] The flooding around Staunton was believed to have been caused mainly by the rain that fell there on Wednesday evening. Within twenty-four hours, Staunton received 9.35 inches, enough to fill the expanded channel for Lewis Creek, which to this day runs through the heart of downtown Staunton. Reports of the damage to the city's municipal infrastructure are prolific. Both the gas and water lines were swept away, leaving one half of the city in darkness and the other without fresh water.[19] The *Staunton Spectator* reported,

> *The water and gas pipes were broken, which had the effect of depriving for a short time, those living East of that place, of water, and those living West, of gas. The West-enders groped in darkness, but quaffed delicious water, the East-enders would have "preferred darkness to light," not "because their deeds were evil," but because, like Coleridge's "Ancient Mariner," with "water, water, everywhere," they had "not a drop to drink."[20]*

STAUNTON—VIEW FROM THE RAILROAD.

Engraving of Staunton from the railroad, circa 1879. *Image taken from* Route, Resorts, and Resources of the Chesapeake and Ohio Railway, of Virginia and West Virginia. *Public domain.*

Partially without water or access to gaslight, a segment of the city's transportation was also lost when the bridge across Main Street succumbed to the rushing water. Several people were standing on the bridge when it collapsed and "a part of the flooring" fell into the stream.[21] Nearly everyone escaped; however, James Teabo was thrown into the water. The newspaper dramatically described it as "being thrown into the very jaws of death, for it was barely possible that his life might be saved."[22] He quickly swept through the channel "like an arrow sped from the bow" and was swiftly carried a half mile before luck allowed him to catch hold of a plank. This small life raft allowed him to hang on until he reached Kayser's Meadow. By the time he was rescued by John Scherer Jr., the twenty-eight-year-old Teabo was exhausted. The paper noted a few days later that "he was much hurt and is still confined to his bed."[23]

Overall, the damage to Staunton was disruptive but could have been much worse. Thankfully, there are no reports of casualties from this location. The *Staunton Spectator* made a point to praise the town council for taking decisive action after a flood from a "heavy Summer shower" in 1860 damaged the business district.[24] The council proactively widened and deepened the channel associated with Lewis Creek. Without this work, the editor of the paper firmly believed that the freshet "would have destroyed utterly the greater part of the business portion of the city" and that "no more judicious expenditure was ever made by the Town."[25] The improvements to the creek helped spare Staunton from the brunt of the flood. However, the surrounding area was not as fortunate.

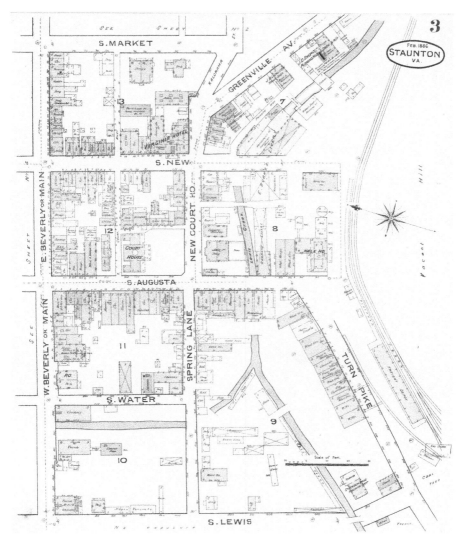

Map depicting how Lewis Creek runs through downtown Staunton. *Library of Congress Digital Archives. Public domain.*

The vicinity around Staunton was confronted with the mass destruction of mills, bridges, houses, fencing, farms, crops and other infrastructure on a scale that rendered it impossible to fully enumerate all instances of loss. At times, the *Staunton Spectator*'s flood coverage read as a succinct damage report, listing known losses of dwellings, mills, bridges and other personal property. Many of those who suffered from the flood had only recently rebuilt or repaired structures and property lost during the Civil War. In an area that suffered directly from the wartime campaigns of David Hunter and Philip Sheridan, the comparison to wartime loss and the flood was a readily available analogy that resonated with much of the populace. Poignantly, a local newspaper pointed out, "The destruction of property caused by this freshet in this county, is vastly more than that caused by the armies—friendly and hostile—during four years of destructive and desolating warfare."[26]

While it is possible that the newspapers overstated this claim, the assertion that the flood either equaled or surpassed the war in terms of property destruction is echoed throughout the Shenandoah Valley in several works. The *Shenandoah Herald* proclaimed that there was a general consensus that the flood was more destructive than the years of war, in an area where six years earlier Ulysses S. Grant had mandated that hard war would be waged to an extent that "crows flying over it for the balance of this season will have to carry their provender with them."[27] The article explained, "From the general account of the late flood in Virginia we learn of the greatest destruction of the crops and property generally, scarcely equaled by the ravages of the late war."[28] In an appeal for aid, the *New York Times* eloquently stressed, "The Valley of Virginia is ravaged as cruelly as though fire and sword had once more visited it; along the James and the Potomac, there is such distress as has not been since the dark days of the rebellion." Although it is possible that the war reference was used as a mechanism for eliciting empathy, the accounts of the damage indicate that the dire situation was not overstated. Many farms, mills and other industries had only recently recovered and would have to rebuild once again after the floodwaters receded. Consequently, the economic burden for some was too much to endure and caused several affected residents to relocate to other areas, file bankruptcy or sell parcels of land.[29]

Moving north along the South River, near Weyers Cave, Susan McCauley's house was swept away. Most of the occupants were able to escape into a grove of trees. However, Mrs. Betsy Ham, who was seventy-nine at the time, was unable to get out of the house before it washed down the river. The *Staunton Spectator* added the grim detail that "her cries could be heard as the house passed points lower down the river."[30] The other nine people in the house, "Mrs. McCauley, two daughters with two babies, two sons and two negro men," made it safely into an arboreous refuge. They clung to the branches throughout the rainy night, unsure if the roots would hold, as the trees "were swayed and shaken by the impetuous torrent" below.[31] Sadly, one of the children did not survive. Although their given names or additional information was not included in the newspaper, census records confirm that Susan McCauley (forty), had six children aged three months to twenty-two along with Mrs. Ham living in her home.[32] The two African American men were likely neighbors. After a harrowing and heartbreaking night, the survivors were rescued the following day.[33]

ROCKINGHAM COUNTY, VIRGINIA

Moving over to the North River in the southern part of Rockingham County, the town of Bridgewater lost its namesake bridge across the waterway. Additionally, the Warm Springs Turnpike was heavily damaged, "being literally washed away in many places."[34] Besides transportation disruptions, the *Staunton Spectator* also reported that mills belonging to George W. Berlin and William Dinkle were swept away. It's likely that damage to the town was extensive but reported only in broad strokes. Vague accounts mention that "a dozen or more houses [were] either totally destroyed or greatly damaged."[35] Unfortunately, there are no names or additional accounts associated with this statement.

In the short span of the river between Bridgewater and Mount Crawford, there was substantial damage to farms. When the water of the North River left the banks, it swept away fencing and corn that was close to harvest. As it reached Mount Crawford, the "fury of the flood" took out the bridge for the town. The Mount Crawford bridge then floated down the river and hit the Valley Turnpike bridge, "causing it to crumble, and both went down together."[36] Between bridge losses and damage to roads, it was estimated that the Valley Turnpike would need approximately $10,000 to cover repairs.[37]

At Grottoes, near the Augusta and Rockingham County line, the Mount Vernon Iron Works were heavily damaged. Initial accounts dramatically inflated the damage: "The Mount Vernon Iron Works, in Rockingham county, are entirely gone, and so are all the tenants' houses."[38] A more restrained account from Staunton noted that the bridge and several buildings belonging to the ironworks were destroyed, which appears to be an accurate assessment.[39] A few weeks later, the *Staunton Spectator* interviewed the owners of the Mount Vernon Iron Works, who estimated that the cost to replace their lost buildings would be between $3,000 and $3,500.[40] They also lost approximately $2,500 in materials. Four years before the flood, the Mount Vernon Iron Works was purchased by the Abbott Iron Company, a Baltimore behemoth employing over 1,100 people and producing $3,500,500 in

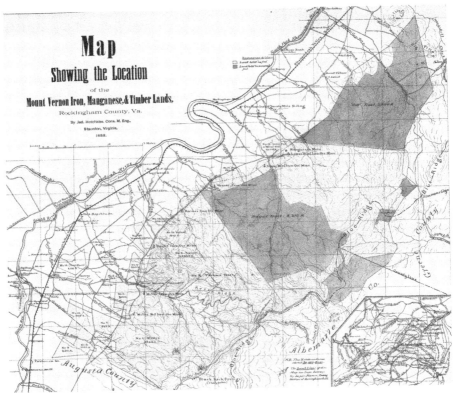

Map of the Mount Vernon Iron Works showing their extensive land holdings, circa 1888. *Library of Congress Digital Archives. Public domain.*

product annually.[41] For an enterprise of that size, not running at full capacity and losing $6,000 in assets is a stark difference from being entirely wiped out. This sort of dichotomy between accounts illustrates how important locating different versions of the story is in order to make the historical assessment as accurate as possible. Even in 1870, a comparison of sources is important to identifying inflated accounts and potentially incorrect news.

PORT REPUBLIC, ROCKINGHAM COUNTY, VIRGINIA

About two miles north of Grottoes, the flood inundated the town of Port Republic at the confluence of the North and South Rivers. Here the rivers merge to become the South Fork of the Shenandoah River. The general accounts of what happened in the town are somewhat vague. The *Alexandria*

Gazette reported that the town was "nearly destroyed."[42] However, accounts from closer to the town succinctly reported, "Some of the buildings, we learn, in Port Republic were destroyed, and other were partially submerged."[43] A later account in the *Rockingham Register* asserted that the town "suffered very little," but the "country immediately around the town suffered incalculably."[44]

By either newspaper or word of mouth, Amanda Petefish "heard that there was great destruction" in Port Republic and "that the whole town washed away, except 4 or 5 houses." On October 10, Petefish wrote a worried letter to her sister Mary Downs, who lived in Port Republic at the time of the flood. Having received little specific information, Petefish, who lived about thirty miles away in Page County, was desperate to know the fate of her family. She wrote, "Is it true[?] Is your property saved and all your lives[?] Have all our family and relations escaped a watery grave? Write to me and let me know."[45] Without knowing how they fared, she offered them a place to stay if they had "been so unfortunate as to lose [their] homes." She also mentioned that she would have written sooner but "thought there was no mail up the river way."[46]

This letter illustrates how difficult it was to obtain information, even from a relatively short distance of thirty miles away. In the wake of the destruction with damaged roads, bridges and a mail service that may have stopped running for a few days, it seems to have taken around two weeks for the sisters to contact each other after the flood. The delay in information seems almost incomprehensible between calling, texting or having access to nearly immediate news from the internet. Correspondence like this also reveals the importance of newspaper accounts for receiving information outside of one's immediate town. The most detailed information often came in the form of letters reprinted in newspapers. This is true of what we know of the flood in Port Republic. The best account of what was happening near there comes from a letter written by Senator John F. Lewis and subsequently published in the *Rockingham Register*.

According to Senator Lewis, the freshet below Port Republic struck the area so quickly that those close to the river were caught off guard. It was raining heavily on Thursday, September 29. As a result, many in the area were preparing for the river to rise a bit. A.L. Wagner, the miller for Senator Lewis's mill, started moving goods stored on the first floor of the mill to the upper levels. While he was working on this task, "the water rose so fast as to cut him and the families living on the banks of the river, off from the hills, [since] the ground upon which the mill and dwelling houses stand being much higher than the land nearer the hills."[47] Although they were on higher

Portrait of John Francis Lewis, a Virginia senator at the time of the flood. His letter to the *Rockingham Register* gives the most detail about the flood at Port Republic, Virginia. *Library of Congress Digital Archives. Public domain.*

ground, the topography immediately around them was lower and rapidly filling with water so that they were cut off from the hills above. Realizing their situation, "they…became alarmed."[48]

Samuel Wagner, who operated a machine shop beside the mills, started building a boat to help them escape to higher ground. Unfortunately, the river was rising so fast at this point that the water reached the door of his shop before he could finish it. In the letter, Senator Lewis emphasized that the water reaching the door of the machine shop was already "four feet above any freshet known up to that time."[49] By this point, the river was raging and full of debris from Staunton, Bridgewater, Grottoes and other places that feed into the South Fork watershed. The boat, unfinished and "rude" as it was, would have to do.

Samuel Wagner and Daniel S. Lewis, Senator Lewis's son, attempted to save an unidentified African American family who must have lived close to the mill. Braving the "angry current," they made it to them in the hastily constructed boat.[50] Sadly, their plan was foiled both by the "strength of the current" and the unfinished boat.[51] The wording is vague, but it appears that the boat was unable to hold much more than the two men without completely foundering. Lewis and Wagner then assisted helping the family into a tree, which they believed was the next-safest option. The family in the tree included "a woman, her two children and two men."[52] There was also a girl who was so frightened by the circumstances "that she could not support herself in the tree." After the remaining members of the family were situated in the tree, Lewis, Wagner and the frightened child "set out on their perilous voyage" and reached the yard of Lynnwood, the home of Senator Lewis, "about a half a mile from the mill."[53]

Back toward the river, A.L. Wagner left his house to get some wood. He ventured about fifteen yards before "the rapidity" of the rising river cut off his return. After he was separated from his house, he joined the family in their temporary tree haven. From their perch in the tree, the refugees held on for dear life as the girth of the river grew from about one hundred yards wide to be "a mile and a quarter."[54] By this time, the Shenandoah River had already become so full of debris that the people in the tree remained in constant fear "of being swept down in the current, the driftwood, hay-stacks, and floating houses threating to bear down the tree in which they had taken refuge."[55] The swift velocity of the rushing waters made the debris into dangerous projectiles that could easily destroy anything in their path, including the tree that had become a tiny island of refuge for six people.

In his letter to the *Rockingham Register*, Senator Lewis also reveals that he and his family were trapped in their house "surrounded by water four to six feet deep" and powerless to help those clinging to the tree. He professed that hearing the "cries of the women and children" trapped in the tree and being unable to render assistance "added to the agonies" of his family.[56] The senator also remarked that on his property alone he "lost over four miles of fencing, five hundred bushels of wheat, between sixty and one hundred tons of hay, five head of fine cattle, between thirty and forty hogs, twenty or thirty barrels of flour, two or three hundred bushels of oats, and nearly all my corn."[57] While unable to save the majority of his livestock, his son Daniel at one point swam to the barn and retrieved eight workhorses and several "very fine thorough breds [sic]," which were housed in the Lewises' dining room for the remainder of the flood. Despite the property loss, the senator, his family and those who lived on his property were lucky in that "no human lives were lost on [the] premises."[58]

The account from Rockingham County reveals the stark disparity of how those living with extreme socioeconomic differences dealt with and encountered the flood. It is hard to imagine a more striking contrast than one between an elected U.S. senator and a family whose name was not even mentioned.[59] Differences of wealth, race, educational access, employment and notoriety all played a role in how each family experienced the flood, its aftermath and their ability to express their personal experiences to the world outside of their immediate community. Since Senator Lewis was an elected representative of the voting populace, he was obviously well known and able to easily add his voice to the printed accounts of the flood by submitting a letter to his local newspaper. Conversely, the African American family's experience was brought to the attention of *Rockingham Register* readers through

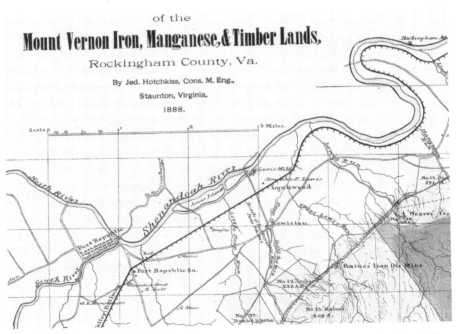

Detail of the Mount Vernon Iron Works map showing the distance between Port Republic, Lynnwood (the home of John Francis Lewis) and Lewis Mill, where A.L. Wagner and a family waited out the flood in a tree. *Library of Congress Digital Archives. Public domain.*

a secondhand account that failed to even recognize their names. Their marginalization is part of a larger pattern that ignored African Americans accounts of the flood. Although they were mentioned and acknowledged as victims of flood events, there is not a single extant firsthand account that originates directly from an African American source.

Additionally, the physical dwelling locations of the Lewis family and the African American family reveal a lot about how location and space interacted with socioeconomic status. The placement of their respective houses seems to have fit within unwritten societal norms. As such, Senator Lewis and his family lived on higher ground, which is often consistent with a wealthier status. Conversely, the African American family lived closer to the water in an area that was more susceptible to the flood. Often laborers and working-class people lived closer to waterways and experienced higher rates of property loss from flooding events. This is especially true in Richmond, where most of the loss was experienced in Rocketts Landing, which was mainly inhabited by African Americans, immigrants and the working class.

The physical location of the dwellings also provided the two families with varying degrees of choices for how to deal with the flood. Since the African American family was quickly inundated by the floodwaters, they had little time to escape with their lives and did not have the opportunity to prepare for the flood. On the other hand, the Lewis family had the luxury of remaining in their house due to the higher topography. The higher ground also granted them extra time and the opportunity to make choices, which helped to save specific livestock. As a result, at least ten horses were saved. This event alone denotes several privileges and elements associated with socioeconomic status, including extensive wealth, which helped to ameliorate the economic aftermath of the flood. Those with greater access to wealth generally got along better than individuals who had fewer available resources. Without knowing the name of the African American family, it is impossible to know how they fared in the post-flood world.

RIVER BANK, ROCKINGHAM COUNTY, VIRGINIA

Between Port Republic and Island Ford in Rockingham County was a small hamlet called River Bank.[60] Here we encounter another tale of a house being washed away. However, it should be noted that the media took a moment to recognize a very good dog. When the water came rushing down the river, the Barker family, along with their dog, Jack, evacuated. However,

Jack ran back into "the dining room to guard the property."[61] The house ended up washing away, and "when the dining room floated off, Jack went with it."[62] To the relief of Mr. Barker and his family, Jack "was found [the] next day about half a mile below River Bank, in the midst of the 'wreck of matter,' guarding his master's property!"[63] Although the Barker family had to rebuild, Mr. Barker declared "that no money can buy this faithful dog."[64] Although a first name is not given in the articles, it's very likely that this was Henry Barker's dog. Henry was a wealthy forty-eight-year-old miller and lawyer that lived at River Bank. On the detail of the map showing the location of River Bank, Dr. Sellers is the only resident mentioned by name. Since Dr. Theodore Sellers is the next head of household on the 1870 census after Henry Barker, it's likely that this is the correct family.[65]

In the midst of the destruction, there are only a few instances where pets are mentioned. Unfortunately, almost assuredly some met terrible ends, but it's heartwarming to know that this family was reunited and that the story was deemed important enough to be reprinted in several newspapers.[66] On the more insidious side, it's another example of how wealth and privilege dictate the stories that we know about the flood. In 1870, Henry Barker's wealth was listed as $10,000 for real estate and $1,275 for personal property.[67] Even though Jack was a good dog, it's likely that newspapers would not have covered this story if the Barker family was poor.

CONRAD'S STORE ROCKINGHAM COUNTY, VIRGINIA

Near the hamlet of Conrad's Store, now the town of Elkton, a Mr. and Mrs. Hertley, who lived about half a mile from the river, were caught completely off guard when their house was "surrounded by water."[68] Realizing they were in immediate danger, they barely escaped on horseback. The brief article eliminates Mrs. Hertley's role or agency in the situation, reducing her to a person who was just put behind her husband on horseback. It's unclear if she survived, as the blurb ends with Mr. Hertley having to "swim for his life."[69] Aside from this story, Conrad's Store lost its bridge and dealt with destroyed fields and the loss of some structures. In this vein, the *Richmond Daily Dispatch* also informed readers that Henry Harnsberger (forty-three) lost a large crop of corn and a tenant house on his property that was occupied by Lorenzo Yager (twenty-six).[70] From this limited information, it appears that the damage was not as concentrated as what would occur a few miles down the river at the Shenandoah Iron Works.

SHENANDOAH IRON WORKS, PAGE COUNTY, VIRGINIA

About seven miles down the river from Conrad's Store, the Shenandoah Iron Works was on the verge of an industrial boom. The former iron plantation was purchased by a group of industrialists who were working to build a modern, profitable industrial complex after the Civil War. At this point, the small town was in an early stage of growth and was about to be reshaped by massive flooding. Here, the South Fork of Shenandoah River abuts steep, rocky banks on the western shore with a smoother floodplain and river islands along the eastern shore. Since the ironworks was originally built on the river islands and along the floodplain to make efficient use of the access to water help fuel and cool the furnace, the settlement was situated at a much lower elevation than the current town of Shenandoah.

Around five o'clock in evening of September 29, the river "reached the top of the bank."[71] This was the "highest point" it had reached in the recollection of anyone living there.[72] The *Rockingham Register* noted that "a few buildings" had already "washed away, but they were unimportant."[73] A concerned citizen stuck a stick "in the bank at the water's edge" to monitor the rise of water, and after a half an hour with no observable rise, it was believed that "the water had reached its height" and there would be no further danger.[74] It was fortunate that Louisa Boude did not maintain a false sense of security and instead remained vigilant and proactive.

Boude noticed "the water coming into her yard, left the house and went to the store with her family and asked to be taken out in a boat."[75] At that point, all the boats were gone except one that "had not been in the river for several months." Thus began a quest to find oars. The only pair of oars located in that vicinity was found in "a cellar a few minutes before the cellar filled with water."[76] If Louisa Boude had waited with her request, it's likely that Shenandoah would have experienced several casualties.

Mrs. Boude and her household, including three-year-old son Rudolph, were taken out of the flooded area in the boat. At the time, Louisa Boude was twenty-nine years old and married to Reverend Adam Poe (A.P.) Boude, a Methodist minister.[77] With her evacuation, the Mason and Deacon families became acutely aware of the pending danger. These families were also extracted by boat as quickly as possible. The water rose so quickly that the Deacon family was "boated out over the top of his yard fence."[78] About a half hour after Louisa Boude left her house, "the water reached the second story."[79]

By 9:00 p.m., the bell of the carpenter's shop was tolling its last. Mr. Stalling, the German painter who was likely working on the ceiling fresco

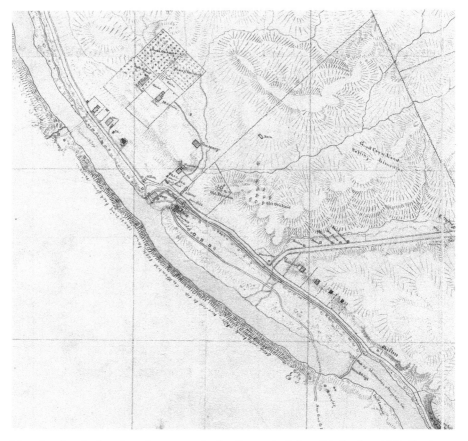

Map showing the location of structures in the Shenandoah Iron Works circa 1865. By the time of the flood, there were more buildings, but nearly all was lost in the floodwaters. *Library of Congress Digital Archives. Public domain.*

for the almost completed Methodist church, was gasping in disbelief at the destruction and sound of the "bell tolling out above the awful roaring of the waters and the crashing of buildings."[80] Daylight revealed that "about thirty buildings were swept away, including the forge, mill, store, Masonic Hall, stables, and the residences of a dozen or more families."[81]

In addition to carrying away buildings and sturdy structures like the forge, the force of the flood was strong enough to swipe and hide the Shenandoah Iron Works' corporate iron safe, which weighed approximately three tons.[82] The safe was carried off and not found until around December 12, even though the company had issued a one-hundred-dollar reward to anyone who found it. Three lucky men stumbled upon it while "gigging fish" and noticed a corner of it with "the rest buried in the sand."[83] It proved almost impossible to retrieve, with several men trying for a week. At first, they attempted to dig it out of the sand, "but having to work in water up to their necks, made slow progress."[84] The following week it was reported that "it remains almost as deeply in the sand as when found." In their attempts, the workers broke "a very large rope and log chain, and also drowned one of their finest mules" because it was unable to pull it out of the muck and drowned during the process.[85] Reports of the safe saga end there. It's unclear how the ironworks finally retrieved it, but an 1871 deed notes that an original deed was "unfit to be recorded" because the paper was so damaged in the flood.[86]

With most everything being swept away, the Shenandoah Iron Works was also suddenly unprepared for the 1870 election. The voter registration books were lost in the flood, and since there were "no duplicates of the same in existence," the Virginia legislature had to pass special legislation "authorizing a new registration."[87] The emergency legislation was passed on October 19 and gave the Shenandoah Iron Works registrar five days to notify voters that they must re-register. After that time, they "shall complete the said registration by the fifth day of November next."[88] At the time, William H. Milnes Jr., one of the owners of the ironworks, was a sitting congressman, having assumed office in January 1870. He opted not to run for reelection "under any circumstances" about a month prior to the flood, with the announcement going out in early September.[89] The local party scrambled to find a candidate. In the end, John T. Harris of Harrisonburg ran unopposed and served in Congress until 1881.

Prior to the flood, it appears that Milnes and his business partners had ambitious plans for the Shenandoah Iron Works, and he may not have wanted to divide his attention. Just two days before the flood, the *Staunton Spectator* announced that the Shenandoah Iron Works would be greatly expanding its operations by erecting "rolling mills, nail factories, &c." The company also announced that with this expansion it was organizing into a joint-stock company.[90]

Everything changed within the span of a few days. The town lost most, if not all, existing structures; the company safe with important documents and whatever cash on hand was missing; and one of the chief architects of the expansion was taken ill with pneumonia. John Fields, who had taken over the company's daily business operations, got "caught in the torrential rains" while he was in Harrisonburg on business.[91] He was fifty-three at the time and did not recover, passing away on November 8, 1870.[92]

Portrait of William Milnes Jr., one of the owners of the Shenandoah Iron Works. Milnes was a congressman at the time of the flood but declined reelection in order to devote all of his energy to what would become the town of Shenandoah. *Image used with permission of the Shenandoah Heritage Society.*

Despite the literal smashing of their dreams, Milnes and his remaining business partners attempted to forge on. According to a company booklet, they were able to begin rebuilding and resume some operations in April 1871 by utilizing their available capital and the labor of their localized workforce.[93] Through a combination of tenacity, access to capital and likely some political and social connections, the town would rebuild and try again.

SLABTOWN AND NEWPORT, PAGE COUNTY, VIRGINIA

A few miles downriver from the Shenandoah Iron Works, the hamlet of Slabtown was almost completely obliterated, "the mills and all the dwellings—six or eight in number—were lost."[94] A letter from Shenandoah did not report the names of those who lost their homes, only "that they saved nothings from their houses, and barely escaped in time to save their lives."[95] This flood essentially wiped Slabtown off the map. In trying to even locate it, only one undated hand-drawn map appears to exist.[96] At Newport, near the current Page County High School, several houses were destroyed, and two thousand bushels of grain were washed away. The losses in this area alone were estimated to be at least $12,000. Several families in both Slabtown and Newport were left homeless and destitute and received little aid to help rebuild their lives.[97] While the flood was devastating to those who lived there, the accounts of the destruction in these areas take up only a few lines of contemporary newspaper coverage, likely indicating that there was so much damage to talk about that it was difficult to cover everything that happened, especially since the tragedy that took place in Honeyville eclipsed everything else in this vicinity.

HONEYVILLE, PAGE COUNTY, VIRGINIA

Continuing down the river, near the current town of Stanley in Page County, the hamlet of Columbia Mills was about to be forever changed. At that time, it was a bustling little community with "a large merchant mill, dwellings, [a] storehouse, used as a dwelling, and other necessary buildings, which denoted prosperity."[98] A few stories survive from this area that illustrate not only the tragic devastation of the flood but also how this community came together in a time of crisis.

On Thursday, September 29, Bertrand W. Petty, a twenty-six-year-old clerk in one of the stores in this area, walked home from work and became acutely aware of the water rising across the lowlands near the river.[99] In order to make it to his house, he was "compelled to walk on the fence" to "get over the low ground, which was covered with water."[100] However, once he was home, assuming that his house and family were safe, he continued his normal routine.

The Petty family went to bed around 9:00 p.m. Although the rain was coming down in a "steady downpour," they "were not disturbed by the continual roar of the mad waters."[101] Around midnight Bertrand, Mary (twenty), their son Herbert (nine months) and Mary's sister Elizabeth Step (eighteen) were awakened by their neighbor Charles Rogers, who alerted them that "the river was rising very fast" and there was no way they would be able to "escape to the high ground" to the east because the rushing water "forced its way over the dam at the bend in the road above."[102] He urged them to come to the storehouse over which the Rogers family lived. By that point, the water was literally at their front doorstep. The Pettys quickly dressed and left through the back door leading to the garden. In the short time it took them to prepare, they were then "stepping out into water knee deep."[103]

Wading through the water, they successfully made their way to the storehouse, outside of which a boatload of 125 to 150 barrels of flour was tethered to the building. Alfred Kite and Robert Aleshire spent the earlier part of the day loading barrels into the boat, which was ready to go to market. As the water rose, they kept moving it up until it eventually reached the rear of the storehouse. Once inside, the Pettys, along with a few other members of the community that had taken refuge there, began moving everything from the first floor to the second, leaving only a cooking stove on that level.[104]

Eleven people watched the water rise by the "faint light of a lantern"; after it reached the steps, "higher and higher it came," until they knew they needed to evacuate to the boat, which was accessible through a window that was quickly becoming in danger of being under water. The party waded through the water on the first floor and then climbed onto the cooking stove to escape through the window into the boat.[105] The entire load of flour was thrown overboard, except for one barrel. Within minutes, the boat's cargo changed to a "freight of souls," including Bertrand, Mary and Herbert Petty, Elizabeth Step, Jarvis Martin, Jack Stoneberger, Alfred Kite, Robert Aleshire, Charles Rogers and his wife and daughter. According to Bertrand Petty, "It seemed like only a few moments until those who were holding the boat to the window gave the unwelcome tidings that the house was moving from its foundation."[106] Knowing that the storehouse was about to give way, they "cut the boat adrift," and "within a few moments," they were "launched onto the boiling and seething flood."[107]

Their journey down the river lasted only a few minutes. With Alfred Kite at the bow and Robert Aleshire at the stern, the two boatmen did their best to guide the vessel through the treacherous waters. According to Petty, "Either the current or the steering caused us to pass near the western shore of the river and it is well we did, for the large sycamores standing at the time along the eastern bank…would have prevented us from passing in safety."[108] The current moved them so swiftly that "it seemed but a moment."[109] Suddenly, Alfred Kite's "oar struck the drift that had formed along the original bank of the river"; the force of the sudden stop threw him "several feet into the water, thus causing the boat to swing around, going over him, when he scrambled to the drift."[110] As luck would have it, "when the boat swung around the bow caught under the end of a large log projecting from the drift and the force of the water kept it in place until all were safely landed." Then in the twinkling of a moment, the boat was smashed to splinters.

A few members of the party began to inspect the trees to which the drift was attached. The first thought was to get all eleven people into the trees, which may have been safer than the drift. However, within moments of the refugees exploring this idea, a few of the trees "were torn down by the force of the water and drift." In the darkness, the cry of "My God" let the party know that they had lost two of their members. Since Jack Stoneberger and Alfred Kite were swept off into the dark gloom, their fates remained unknown for several days. Sadly, this was where Jack Stoneberger met his end. The rest of the party steeled themselves on the drift, which rose and fell "on each side as if it were on a pivot."[111] In stressed terror, they waited out the night "not knowing whose lot it would be next" and trying to put their faith in he "who rules the Tempest."[112] All they could do was "watch and wait" until finally "the faint streaks of light in the east" revealed that they made it through the night, which started to allow "some room for hope" into their hearts.[113]

In the same vicinity, Noah and Isabella Kite were hosting two guests at their Honeyville home, their recently married daughter, Elenora Nauman, and Augustus West, a carpenter from Richmond who was in the area purchasing southern bank notes for a Richmond firm.[114] Noah Kite was a well-known merchant miller and farmer whose industry helped build the Columbia Mills hamlet. The Kites lived close to the modern Alma Bridge on Business Route 340 in Page County. Their house was a sturdy dwelling with an original two-story frame structure and a brick addition. It was situated on the top of a natural hill that had not been threatened by floodwaters during their lifetimes.

Since his home was not historically in danger from previous floods, Noah Kite believed that everything would be all right and decided not to evacuate. An account from the *Shenandoah Valley* newspaper claimed, "He [Noah Kite] had seen high water before and feared no danger."[115] With the assumption of safety, the family and their guests ate dinner and proceeded with their visit. In addition to their guests, the Kites still had five children living at home, along with twenty-year-old William Martin, who was working as a farm laborer and listed as a part of the household on the 1870 census.[116] Not long after sunset, the Kites' thirteen-year-old son, George, decided that he would prefer to spend the night in the barn. His parents acquiesced to this wish, and George left the house with William Martin. Together they waded to the brick barn with their blankets through water that was "then more than waist deep."[117]

Under the cover of darkness, the water rose with fury. The sliver of light from the moon had not yet reached the first quarter following a new moon earlier in the week. The dearth of natural light may have contributed to complacency when the creeks, streams and rivers overflowed their banks later that evening.[118] By the time the Kites were aware of the extent of the rising waters, retreat was "wholly cut off."[119] Some of the outbuildings, "including the distillery and the stone spring-house, had already been swept away."[120] Rain pelted the exterior of the house, and soon the inside would fail to be a haven from the elements.

As the first floor filled with water, Noah Kite sat at the top of the stairs with a lantern watching the water rise with such rapidity that it seemed like every minute another tread became covered with water.[121] Soon, the second-floor refuge was also submerged, and the inhabitants squeezed into the garret attic space. As the deafening roar of the Shenandoah River at flood stage engulfed the house, all they could do was hope and pray that the foundation would hold steady.

Close to midnight, near the time that the Petty family was being awakened, the mortar and stones of the foundation and the chimneys began to give way and the house was lifted from its footing. When the middle chimney collapsed, "they felt the house surge and give way."[122] As the house was dislodged from its permanent location, the brick addition collapsed. Then, the older frame structure was pulled down the river as a floating entity. Noah Kite, fifty-six at the time, punched a hole in the roof and started lifting his wife and children onto the rooftop. Most accounts agree that Isabella (forty-seven), Erasmus (twenty), Ashby (seven) and Edward (five) all escaped onto the roof before the attic and second floor collapsed, likely killing Noah, Elenora (twenty-five), Eudora (sixteen) and Augustus West (sixty-two) in the process. For several minutes, the roof swept down the river under fierce force, in utter darkness and pouring rain. At a high velocity, the roof "struck a drift" and was smashed into several pieces.[123] The remaining family members were scattered and struggled to hold on. The piece that Isabella, Edward and Ashby were gripping was swept under the waves and lost.

Erasmus saw that the piece of roof that he was clinging to was in peril and desperately tried to reach out to passing trees for refuge. By luck, he passed a floating log and jumped to it. With the aid of driftwood, he swam about three-quarters of a mile before he reached a haystack "that had lodged" against a tree or drift.[124] Alone in the dark with only the shirt on his back, he climbed onto the haystack and started digging for dry straw. As luck would have it, the center of the haystack was dry. Erasmus, cold, soaking wet and nearly naked, "burrowed into it, fell asleep, and slept till late next day."[125] When the dawn came, Erasmus found himself two and a half miles downriver in the bottomland of Phillip Long's farm.[126]

Map of the Shenandoah Valley, circa 1860s. Detail depicting the distance between Newport, Honeyville, Alma and White House. This image also shows the location of Phillip Long's farm, where Erasmus Kite ended up after journeying down the Shenandoah River. *Library of Congress Digital Archives. Public domain.*

Daybreak set the scene for the needed rescue of eleven people from Columbia Mills. If one were able to get a bird's-eye view of the river, Erasmus Kite would be sleeping in a haystack, Alfred Kite in the top of a locust tree and nine members of the party that left the storehouse in a boat, stuck on a bobbing drift near the original riverbank. Petty recalled, after dawn broke, "It was not long before lights began to appear at the residence of Mr. Isaac Long which occupied the high ground east of us by his barn, and by waving our hats and handkerchiefs, let them know our location. They soon recognized our signals."[127] The river was so high and wide at that point that it took a lot of logistics and discussion from those gathered on the riverbank to decide what to do. From Bertrand Petty's account, those on the drift could see folks gathered on the shore, but were far enough away that verbal communication was impossible. That alone illustrates how the river had exponentially expanded outside of its banks.

The folks on the drift had the benefit of watching what the crowd was doing; however, it's unclear if Erasmus Kite was able to make his presence known or see the efforts from his location. Around 10:00 a.m., those on the drift saw the people on shore "hitch horses to a wagon" and guessed that they were heading to get lumber to build a boat.[128] This guess was verified by the wagon's return. For "several hours," they watched as the boat was constructed. In the afternoon, the boat was carried several yards above the drift, and John Flannery and Dan Kite, Alfred's brother, got in and endeavored to rescue them. The still-rushing current prevented them from getting nearer than fifty yards. At this point, Jarvis Martin and Robert

Aleshire "waded out below the drift as far as they could" and then let themselves float with the tide toward the boat. They both made it to the boat, which then started for the shore. The current was swift, thus thwarting a safe landing near a wooded ridge. When they were close to shore, but moving too quickly to stop, Dan Kite jumped off the bow and made it onto land. Robert Aleshire followed his lead, but Dan's jump pushed the boat a little too far and Aleshire fell into the swift current. As the river carried him, he attempted to catch hold of a limb, but "not having strength enough or the weakness of the limb prevented him from reaching the shore and he was drowned."[129] Flannery and Martin continued to drift with the boat around the point and soon landed safely.

From the movement on land, those on the drift realized that there was someone in the trees below them. After a while, the boat set out on a second rescue attempt, this time with just John Flannery, as Dan Kite had exhausted his strength on the first attempt. The boat could get no closer than before; as a result, Flannery attempted to rescue Alfred Kite in the trees below. Flannery successfully got Alfred into the boat, and they partook of "some refreshments."[130] Suddenly, the boat was caught by a strong current and swept away, "throwing both into the water."[131] They both made it into trees near each other but were forced to spend the night there. The treacherous waters meant that only one person was rescued, one died and ten people remained in peril Friday night.

The water started to recede Friday afternoon, which then added a new concern for the seven people on the drift. Since the water was holding it up, would the drift break apart or become unsound during the night? After examining the water, they determined that they "could rest with some security."[132] The three women had wrapped themselves in "some bed clothes" when they left the house, and a featherbed that they were sitting on in the second story of the storehouse somehow ended up on the drift ahead of them.[133] They used these items to make the drift a bit more comfortable and get some rest in shifts. Petty noted, "Some say, how can you sleep? My only answer is—let them undergo the same and tired Nature will seek relief in sweeter sleep than they ever had or will enjoy."[134]

The drift also had its share of other inhabitants. During the day, "it seemed every kind of insect and reptile" collected on this small respite from the water. However, the "terrors of the previous night had made them as humble we were," and they "soon sought one end" and "we the other."[135] The biodiversity and natural impact is often overlooked, but it's important to realize that the flood had an immeasurable effect on ecosystems near the river.

When the folks on the drift awoke, they could see that the water had significantly receded and that "there was land in many places" underwater the night before. A group of people, including John Seakford, started the rescue efforts around 8:00 a.m.[136] They first rescued John Flannery and Alfred Kite from the trees and landed on shore. Next, they returned for the people on the drift, who "waded out as far as [they] could to meet them." After being successfully rescued, they were grateful to reach land and be provided with dry clothes and breakfast. They only thing they had been able to eat while on the drift were apples retrieved from the nasty floodwaters.[137] Erasmus Kite was also rescued around this time. Clothed in just his shirt, soaked and exposed to the elements, he remained in the haystack until the floodwaters receded enough for him to be rescued on Saturday morning.[138] Their harrowing thirty-six hours of danger were over thanks to neighbors who came together to build boats, brave the waters and provide immediate basic necessities.

By the dawn of Saturday, October 1, twenty-year-old Erasmus had lost his parents, two sisters and two brothers, along with his home and family milling business. In addition, he became the legal guardian of his younger brother, George, and the executor of his parents' estate. In accordance with the law, the remaining personal property associated with the estate was sold at auction only a month after the freshet.[139] The shock of losing so many relatives and having a personal brush with death in one evening was visible to all who knew him. Local residents claimed that after the flood, his hair began to turn gray and he started to lose his youthful appearance. The psychological strain in this instance manifested in a physically visible way. While Erasmus did not produce a written account of the events in his own words, after his rescue, he was greeted by approximately one hundred people who listened intently to his heartbreaking tale and documented the occurrence.[140] Accounts of the family tragedy were detailed in multiple newspapers across the region and cover about eight pages of Harry Strickler's *A Short History of Page County*.[141] Bertrand Petty's account was printed later in his life, after he received notoriety serving in the Virginia House of Delegates. It was also included in Strickler's book but was not a significant part of the media portrayal at the time of the flood. The story concerning the loss of the Kite family continued to live in the public memory of the surrounding area and led to the construction of a memorial near the Kite farm in 1938.

Augustus H. West's fate became known to his family about a week after the flood. According to articles in the *Richmond Enquirer* and the *Rockingham Register*, West purchased a horse in Page County the day before he visited

Noah Kite. He also left a letter for his wife in the care of the seller. The *Rockingham Register* noted, "The first intimation had of his fate was the horse's return to his old owner."[142] News of his death, along with his last letter, reached his wife, Sarah West, and their six children, all of whom were still living at home, during the week following the flood.[143] Receiving that final communication in conjunction with the terrible news must have been heartbreaking.

WHITE HOUSE, PAGE COUNTY, VIRGINIA

About seven miles as the river flows from Alma is an unincorporated community known as White House. Named for a Rhenish stone house built by Martin Kauffman II in 1760, it became a landmark of the area, with its name deriving from the white stucco exterior that was likely added in the early nineteenth century.[144] At the time of the flood, the area included the White House, Augustus S. Modisett's dry goods store, a few dwellings, a toll house and a new turnpike bridge—all of which were affected by the floodwaters.

The toll gate house near the White House Bridge was lived in and operated by Joel Price. The raging waters swept the building away, along with Price, who remained in the house until it was pulled from the foundation.[145] Then, he swam out and was able to get to an elm tree. The community searched for him until around noon on Friday and began to despair, thinking he was lost. When they were close to giving up, "he was found about 100 yards below his house" and rescued from the branches of the elm tree on Friday the thirtieth, which also happened to be his seventy-first birthday.[146]

The bridge that spanned the river at this point was owned by the New Market and Sperryville Turnpike Company. According to the *Staunton Spectator*, it "stood eighteen feet above the ordinary bed of the river," and the water ran "at least twelve feet over it."[147] The newspaper estimated that the river reached at least thirty feet above the normal level at this point. The turnpike company opted not to rebuild this bridge until 1910, when it was replaced with an iron bridge costing $20,000.[148] For the next forty years, crossing the river in that location depended on a ferry or fording the river.

Close to this area, Modisett's dry goods and grocery was heavily damaged, with most of the stock ruined and "the house being destroyed." John Mauck, who was managing it, "lost his all."[149] Although the details are vague, Mauck was lauded for rescuing two or three people at great peril to his own life.[150]

Built by Martin Kauffman II in 1760, this Rhenish stone house with white stucco has been a landmark in Page County for 260 years. *Image used with the permission of the White House Farm Foundation.*

The floodwaters reached the stone house known as Locust Grove, which is situated on the north bank of Massanutten Creek. At the time, Harvey C. and Ann M. Strickler and their family lived in the house. Mr. Strickler wrote in a letter that the water reached the house in a wave or "single swell" of about seven feet. The family rushed to the second floor and waited out the flood in the old stone house, which was built in 1760, the same year as the White House. They spend the night in the garret, listening to the "roaring of the raging water and crash of trees and drift outside."[151] If their dwelling had been frame, it likely would have been carried off.[152] The water crested around 3:00 a.m., covering about seven feet of the first floor of the house. The Strickler family was rescued by boat the following day by Paul Hinkle and John Haynes.[153] Although their house survived, they lost about $5,000 in personal property, including livestock, crops, 250 barrels of corn and 400 bushels of wheat. Strickler also noted the heavy flood deposits of sand, including four feet on his lawn and five feet covering the potato patch. These estimates are consistent with the archaeological record of the area.

The floodwaters moved with swift force and carried a lot of debris. In addition to decimating physical structures that lay in its path, it also changed the topography of the land in some instances. According to the *Rockingham Register*, "Extensive portions of the soil of many of the valuable farms on the river front, have been swept off, and the lands utterly, irreclaimably raised."[154] The effects of this phenomenon can be found even today. At the White House, on Route 211 near Luray, the eighteenth-century stone and stucco structure was almost completely engulfed by the floodwaters. During archaeological investigations in 2013 and 2014, the 1870 flood deposit was found in the stratigraphy surrounding the house. While varying slightly in depth, the 1870 flood deposit in this area is approximately eight inches of sandy sediment that was possibly deeper at the time of the flood.[155] This amount of deposit would have been nearly impossible to remove from fields and likely altered much of the landscape adjacent to the river, burying and, conversely, scouring the soil in different areas. This likely had a profound effect on parts of the Shenandoah Valley agricultural community, since the altered land surface probably affected the 1871 crop yields.

WARREN COUNTY

Continuing into Warren County, the waterways wreaked havoc as the destruction swept north along the winding path of the South Fork of Shenandoah River. A letter to the *Alexandria Gazette* described damage to the farms and mills along the river in the southern part of the county, near Bentonville. It appears that this small community was left with only "one barrel of corn" after the waves of destruction swept through the area.[156] At the end of September, the corn crop in the floodplains along the river was ready for harvest. In Bentonville, it had been cut but was still in the fields awaiting the next step of processing. Suddenly, it was gone, along with the mills to grind it into cornmeal. The author pointedly stated, "There will be hard times in our county this winter, for most of the farmers lost all, even their houses, and have no house to live in, and have no grain to feed their stock on."[157]

FRONT ROYAL, WARREN COUNTY, VIRGINIA

About fifteen miles above Bentonville, the Shenandoah River snakes around Front Royal. Just below the town, several lives were lost when the river reached a height that surpassed all known floods in the area, a recurring theme in this narrative. Situated about fifty-five miles downriver from Stanley, the crest in this area took place almost eight hours after the Kite family tragedy.[158] At dawn on Friday, September 30, the water was still rising in Front Royal when the Blakemore family and their guests were caught off guard by the unprecedented river depth.

A significant amount is known about what happened to the Blakemore family and their house guests on September 30, 1870, because of an account from James Coffman "J.C." Blakemore fifty-five years after the flood. The 1870s newspaper accounts recount some of the broad strokes but nothing like the details and firsthand description of survival that J.C. Blakemore relayed as a seventy-two-year-old man. The awful details of that day burned into Blakemore's mind were retold by John Wayland in his history of Shenandoah County.[159]

The evening of September 29, the Blakemore family received three guests. Newton and Jacqueline Ridgeway, who were recently married over the summer, came to pay their friends a visit. In an unrelated excursion, Barney Kauffman of Page County also stopped there to spend the night.[160] The seven members of the Blakemore family included Thomas (forty-four) and Mary (forty-six) and five children: James C. (seventeen), Nathan (fifteen), Mary H. "Helen" (thirteen), Elzora (eleven) and Flora (six).[161] J.C. Blakemore took special care to reiterate that they were caught unaware and there was not a rise in the river the day before. That Thursday, he "ran the sawmill all day until late in the evening." Since it was located along the water, he noticed that the river "had just begun to swell a little" and was "getting a little muddy" when he quit for the evening.[162]

The next indication that the river was rising happened around 2:00 a.m. A neighbor who came over to check "to see if there were any eels in the fish trap at the mill" woke Thomas Blakemore to alert him that "the river was rising and was nearly up to the mill."[163] Blakemore chose to rest a little longer and got up between three and four o'clock that morning. When he saw the rising water, he woke his sons, J.C. and Nathan, along with Newton Ridgeway and Barney Kauffman, to help move things "out of the mill."[164] After successfully securing everything from the mill, they started to move "the lumber that was on the yard to higher ground."[165] However, every time they finished moving the lumber, the water caught up with them and they had to move it again.[166]

As an aside, J.C. Blakemore mentioned that Jacqueline Ridgeway accompanied her husband downstairs around 4:00 a.m. when they were called to move things out of the mill. When Jacqueline came into Mary

Blakemore's room, Mary asked her, "Why did you get up?"[167] Newton Ridgeway, her husband, "remarked laughing, 'Oh, she is afraid that the water will come up to the room.'"[168] The derision at her fear is unnecessary and dismissive. Had they heeded her fears instead of dismissing them, six lives could have been saved.

As the light of dawn began to show, Thomas Blakemore, whose mills had been burned during the Civil War, got to see the rays of daylight cross his recently rebuilt mills one last time before they were lost to the flood. That morning, "he saw all the fruit of his toil and labor since the war closed, swept from its foundations and carried away." Completely distraught, but unaware of their pending danger, Thomas Blakemore "came into the house exclaiming, 'I am ruined, I am ruined.'"[169] Economic ruin preoccupied his thoughts and actions that morning, which favored saving material goods rather than evacuation, with the assumption that they would be safe in their house on higher ground.

A little before 8:00 a.m., their perilous situation started to become apparent, and Thomas Blakemore became visibly uneasy. He walked toward the nearest neighbor's house, "which was back on the side of the hills across the ravine" and already filled with water.[170] He called to the neighbors and asked if they could make a boat to "come over" and try to get them out.[171] The neighbor responded, "You are not scared are you?" Thomas Blakemore replied, "No, but it is a little worse than I ever saw it."[172] Blakemore owned a larger boat used on the river and a small skiff, but both were tied at the low-water mark and completely out of reach at that point. According to J.C. Blakemore, they had access to plenty of lumber to build a boat, but no nails. Also, as the water was rising so fast, J.C. Blakemore doubted that "they would have had time" to make a boat even if they had nails.[173]

A few minutes later, "the water came with a rush," and everyone was "driven into the house."[174] Thomas Blakemore began preparing the house for a potential journey down the river and a subsequent escape. He removed "all of the sash out of the upstairs windows."[175] Following the rise of the river, J.C. Blakemore's letter vividly described the moments while they waited in tense suspense on the second floor. His father was "standing by or sitting in one" of the windows. His mother, Mary, sat in the floor with her youngest daughter, Flora, in her lap. J.C. recalled, "I do not remember hearing a sound from her [Mary]. I am certain she was engaged in silent prayer."[176] Jacqueline Ridgeway was "frantic with fear and it was taking all of her husband's time keeping her from getting out the window."[177] J.C. Blakemore also described his personal actions: "I had fixed my clothes so that I could get rid of them on a moment's notice, and was lying on the floor praying as I had never prayed before, and I doubt if I have since."[178]

The water rose to the second floor within minutes, and then "the house was lifted from its foundation and carried off."[179] For a few moments, the brick chimney held the house in place, tethering it "until it turned completely around."[180] Barney Kauffman made it out onto the roof of the porch before the house was torn from the foundation, but when the house started down the river, the porch broke off.[181] Kauffman held on to the roof and floated about a mile until he was able to grasp hold of a tree. He was lucky that the tree held and outlasted the flood and was rescued later that evening.[182]

When the house started down the river, Thomas Blakemore said for everyone to move up to the attic, "the stairway of which was in the next room."[183] Thomas, J.C. and Nathan "started for the door," but before J.C. reached it, "the house suddenly went down." The water lifted him "against the ceiling of the room." When the house came back up, J.C. was suddenly alone in the room. However, before he "could make any attempt to get out or do anything, it went down again." The water refilled the room and pressed J.C. to the ceiling. In those terrifying moments, he thought that "it would never come up, and I believe if it had stayed down for half a minute or a minute longer I would not be penning these lines."[184]

As he was at the point of giving up, J.C. recounted that the house "suddenly raised and [I] sprang to a window. Stopping long enough to take my bearings, I found that the house had not yet gone into the main current of the river yet, but was floating along in the bottom land." He waited for the house to pass and "then swam to the hillside, not the shore of the river." Blakemore added, "When I landed I was as naked as I was the day I was born." He started walking toward the home of Daniel Kibler and was met by his son John, who gave him "a pair of pants and a shirt."[185]

While in the water, J.C. heard someone call to him. He turned his head to see Newton Ridgeway and his sister Helen "on top of the house." A moment later, "the house passed out into the main current of the river" and proceeded "under a large sycamore tree." Newton Ridgeway was able to grab "a limb of this tree and saved himself." Around that time, Helen was knocked off the roof and drowned. Elzora managed to get "on a log and went for some fifteen or twenty miles before she was drowned."[186] Local newspapers reported sightings of a girl believed to be Elzora passing Riverton "kneeling upon a bunch of debris, with her arms folded and face turned upward and seemingly unconscious of all around."[187] Riverton is about five miles down the river from where the Blakemores lived. If her brother's estimate is correct, she likely made it to around Morgan's Ford before finally succumbing to exhaustion. That same source also believed that witnesses saw Thomas Blakemore go down the river shortly after Elzora "upon a log."[188] However, that is the last supposed sighting of Thomas Blakemore before he met a watery grave.

That dawn, six lives were lost from this location. The same day, E.A. Wilson and a Dr. Roy manned a boat and rescued Barney Kauffman from the tree. Later, Dr. Roy and Richard Bagly attempted to save Newton Ridgeway. However, they were unable to reach the shore. Roy, Bagly and Ridgeway all spent the night "in a tree which overhung the foaming waters." They were later rescued by E.A. Wilson and Charles Baxter. Although Nathan Blakemore survived, his brother, J.C., doesn't mention the particulars of his escape. A few days later, the *Alexandria Gazette* reported that Jacqueline Ridgeway's body was found buried in the sand near where the Blakemore house stood. Mary Blakemore was found below Riverton, and one of the girls, likely Elzora, was located about fifteen miles below Riverton.[189]

RIVERTON, WARREN COUNTY, VIRGINIA

According to the *Shenandoah Herald*, the flood near this area was reported to be "sixty five feet above the low water mark."[190] The height of the water reached the fifth story of Weston's Mill at the confluence of the North and South Forks of the Shenandoah River north of Front Royal.[191] The intersection of waterways was likely a higher point of water due to the high volume of both rivers and topography. It is the largest contemporary report of high water that has been located. For scale, an image of the mill may help to illustrate the height of the water in the location. Additionally, the water

Riverton Mills, Warren County, Virginia. The flood reached the fifth story of the mill and is an excellent visual reference for imagining the height of the floodwaters. *Image used with the permission of the Laura Virginia Hale Archives and Warren Heritage Society, Warren County, Virginia.*

was reported to be at least sixty feet above the low-water mark at Riverton Station, about two miles west of Front Royal. The flood reportedly swept "over the top" of the Railroad Bridge—which was about sixty feet above the low-water mark—before carrying it off.[192]

NORTH FORK OF THE SHENANDOAH, SHENANDOAH COUNTY, VIRGINIA

Since Riverton is the location where the two forks of the Shenandoah River meet, it's important to also look at what happened along the North Fork, which runs through northern Rockingham County and the length of Shenandoah County. Although there was flooding, the *Shenandoah Herald* explained, "The damage on the North Branch of the Shenandoah is not so great as that of the South Branch."[193] The information about the damage is comparatively sparse. However, broad-stroke descriptions reveal that the "entire corn crop along the North Branch has been swept off. The bottoms of the entire course of the river are entirely inundated, and presented the appearance of vast lakes."[194]

Although fewer specifics are known, a few stories make their way into the media. Near Mount Jackson, Lizzie Allen was reported missing on October 20. At the time, she was staying at the home of her brother Tiphen Allen. It's unclear if she was permanently living there, since she is not listed on the 1870 census as part of the household.[195] The brief article explained, "She was complaining, and had been confined to her room." Obviously frustrated with the current state of her situation, Lizzie went "missing from her room on the night of the flood, and has not been heard from since."[196] This is the only bit of information available on this story. Without a follow-up, it's unknown if Lizzie was ever found or what fate befell her.

Several miles up the river, near Strasburg, Charles D. Chamberlain of Frederick County, Virginia, was lost to the floodwaters when attempting to visit Andrew Pitman on the other side of the river. The twenty-two-year-old was presumed to have drowned when his horse was found on Monday, October 3, "among some drift some distance below the ford."[197] Chamberlain is buried in Winchester with the presumed death date of October 2, 1870.[198]

About two miles from Strasburg, the railroad bridge across the North Fork was "greatly damaged" when "a portion of the trestle work was swept away."[199] Both freight and passenger trains heading west crossed over the bridge shortly before its destruction. The passenger train ended up being stuck at Riverton, "on account of the destruction of the bridge across the South Branch." As previously mentioned, the massive high-water levels swept over the bridge, which was about sixty feet above the low-water mark. The passenger train attempted to return to Strasburg; however, the bridge there was already "too greatly damaged."[200] As a result, both trains were "cut off between the two branches of the Shenandoah."[201]

ISLAND FORD MILLS, WARREN COUNTY VIRGINIA

After Riverton, the combined forks of the Shenandoah continue through the northern portion of Warren County, heading toward Clarke County. Although no longer considered a landmark, Island Ford Mills was heavily damaged. Covered in much less detail than the Blakemores, the family of Henry Hoskins also lost their lives in this vicinity. Living "about a mile and a half above Island Ford Mills," their house was swept away by the floodwaters.[202] The 1870 census records that Mary Hoskins was nineteen at the time. In addition to losing Mary, their ten-month-old son, William, was also lost to the floodwaters. An article in the *Shenandoah Herald* mentioned that Mr. Hoskins's sister-in-law also drowned. However, her name is not included in the census records. So, she was either visiting or had moved in sometime after July 1870. Henry Hoskins, age twenty-four, was the only member of this family that survived; he managed to "grasp hold of some bushes."[203] As a young couple, Henry and Mary were doing well financially with $500 in land holdings and $750 in personal property. However, after the loss of his family and home, it is unknown how Henry rebuilt his life and dealt with this tragedy.

The path of destruction from Lewis Creek in Staunton to the confluence of the North and South Forks of the Shenandoah River in Warren County was immense, causing at least twenty deaths and sweeping away dwellings, mills, bridges and anything within the grasp of the violent waterways. Some towns would never be rebuilt or fully recover, forever changing the landscape of the valley. The raging floodwaters continued to dash along this path, sending waves of destruction into Clarke County and toward Harpers Ferry in West Virginia, leading to "a scene of ruin and desolation" beyond compare.[204]

THE STEM OF THE SHENANDOAH BECOMES A SCYTHE

Clarke County, Virginia, to Washington, D.C.

As far as his astounded eyes could reach, an angry mountain current, alive and wild, leaped over plain and woodland, sweeping everything before it like an avalanche, while the surrounding hills groaned beneath its lashes, making in all a wilder hell than ever he dreamed of. Rising at night with the most fearful rapidity, whole families were whirled, ere they had time to recover from sleep, headlong into the unfathomable depths of that undiscovered country from whose bourn no traveler returns.
—Alexandria Gazette, *October 7, 1870*

Albert sang hymns from the top of the apple tree while waiting for rescue. His attempt to escape from the raging waters at Snicker's Ferry was foiled when his horse fell and he had to scramble to the top of the nearest tree. The wait was tough, and like any person in a life-or-death situation, he asked for help. While continuing to wait and hope, much of his time in the tree was occupied with song and prayer. Help was on the way and close to reaching him when a stable floated down the river and struck the tree. Albert disappeared into the waves, and his fate was unknown after that point.

The *Shepherdstown Register* didn't know Albert's last name but included that he was an African American man. The writer who recorded the story used an important verb. When waiting for rescue, Albert was engaged with "giving out hymns, singing and prayer."[205] Giving out: here was a man facing an uncertain fate and still giving to the world. Whether or not he survived, the sweeping torrent added his voice and experience to those it collected and affected along its treacherous path.

After the forks of the Shenandoah River met near Front Royal, the sweeping torrent of the main stem continued through rural Clarke County before crossing into Jefferson County, West Virginia. Much of the destruction in Clarke County—that we know about—took place near the ferries. There was additional agricultural and mill damage throughout the county, but the largest instances of concentrated damage took place near the veins of travel. Once into West Virginia, the flooding continued along a mainly rural path through Jefferson County before reaching the industrialized city of Harpers Ferry, which became the scene of so much death and destruction that it forever left a mark on the town, reshaping its economic and social landscape. Fifty-seven miles from Riverton in Warren County, the Shenandoah River meets the Potomac at Harpers Ferry, where the flood's path of destruction turned toward Washington, D.C., sending waves of debris down the river and toward the bridges and shores of Georgetown, Washington and Northern Virginia, finally calming as the river widened and the terrain flattened.

BERRY'S FERRY, CLARKE COUNTY, VIRGINIA

The flood continued its destructive path into Clarke County. Along this inevitable trajectory, Berry's Ferry was the first part of this route to be significantly affected, as it had a larger population living along the water. Due to its proximity to the river, "the ferry house at Berry's Ferry" was swept away "and the ferryman drowned."[206] Aside from his profession, the only clue to his identity comes from an article originally printed in the *Clarke Courier* indicating that he was born in Prussia and "named Fritz."[207] This area also lost an elderly African American man named "Robinson."[208] Another letter from Clarke County confirms that "two lives were lost" at this location.[209] In addition to the lives lost, some accounts assert that all of the houses "at Berry's Ferry save one" had been washed away.[210] The dearth of specifics for Berry's Ferry makes it difficult to fully unravel a lot of what happened here, but it appears that this community suffered from the freshet.

A few miles down the river, at the Swift Shoal Mill, a forty-one-year-old miller named John H. Ford worked with his son John (eighteen) and nephew to move "1,500 bushels of wheat" above the rising waters in a mill that was several stories high.[211] By the time they succeeded in moving the wheat to the second level, the water came close to encroaching on their work. After taking the time to move the grain up to another story, John Ford realized that their work was in vain and that their lives were in peril.[212] His first plan was for all of them to swim out and save themselves.[213] However, upon discovering that his nephew couldn't swim and that they would likely be sentencing him to a watery grave, Ford decided that they should wait out the flood. The group remained in the mill until they were positive that the structure was about to give way. As the "furious waters rapidly rose from floor to floor, the three sat coolly and patiently awaiting the pleasure of the devouring flood, which surged and raved around them."[214]

While waiting to meet their fate with dignity, they were unaware that their neighbors were working on building a boat to rescue them. Philip Hansucker and a few others finished the craft just in time and brought it down to the water in a wagon. Two "first rate watermen" named Hilleary Burch and Lewis Wood volunteered to brave the waters and expertly commanded the craft on its rescue mission. One can imagine the surprise and relief that those in the mill felt when they were rescued "from their perilous situation."[215]

CASTLEMAN'S FERRY, CLARKE COUNTY, VIRGINIA

The next community to be hit by a wave of destruction was Castleman's Ferry. Most assuredly, several houses were swept away at this location. According to one account from Richmond, "All the houses (sixteen in number) were driven from their moorings by the surging waves, and the main building of the hotel and storehouse alone left to mark the spot."[216] Without corroborating information, it's hard to know if that account was grossly exaggerated, but other accounts confirm the names of a few of the more prominent sufferers.

Two members of the community—John W. Steel and James W. Jones—were mentioned by name in separate newspaper accounts. The 1870 census records place Steel and Jones on the same page as neighboring households, making it highly likely that these are the same individuals who were referred to as "worthy, excellent men, whose earnings were gained in the sweat of their brows, lost their houses, books, papers—all!"[217] The census also reveals that both were craftsmen. John Steel, age forty-three, was a master blacksmith with an apprentice in his household. James Jones, age forty-nine, appears to have taught the bricklaying trade to his twenty-year-old son, who was still residing at home.

Aside from these limited specifics, one account in the *Shenandoah Herald* mentions that an African American man drowned while "attempting to save some horses belonging to Kemp's Stage Line."[218] His name and age were not given. Without other specifics, it's hard to know if he lived in the area or was itinerantly working with the stage line. As a result, his identity remains a mystery.

A short distance from the community, "above the ferry," the recently completed home of twenty-six-year-old George Copenhaver was "washed away." George and his family were very well off and living on a farm worth $6,020 in real estate and $1,000 personal property. From the 1870 census, George and Virginia (twenty-two) had two small children: two-year-old Mary and one-year-old Huston. There were also able to employ a twenty-year-old domestic servant named Ann Wiley. They were fortunate that all living in their household escaped the flood.

ROCK FORD, JEFFERSON COUNTY, WEST VIRGINIA

Crossing into Jefferson County, John Handcock Berkley Lewis did not encounter that same luck. He lost his life while attempting to retrieve clothing from his home. John was a successful miller by trade. He, Mary and their family had already evacuated their home when the flooding was imminent. Thinking that he had more time, John, who was fifty years old, ran back into the house to gather additional clothing. It was at that inopportune moment that a wave came down the Shenandoah River and washed away his home, located near the Rockford mill, with him in it. His body was "recovered on Saturday, a mile or so down the river."[219] His death marked the first of many recorded fatalities in the terrible flooding that hit Jefferson County and is often included in the count with the casualties at Harpers Ferry.

Several weeks later, Mary Lewis placed a public appeal in the *Spirit of Jefferson* newspaper. Of all the things they lost, she was trying to find two trunks with their initials on them. Her trunk was yellow with the initials M.E.K., while John's is described as a "hand trunk marked J.H.B.L."[220] After losing all of their worldly goods, finding a bit of home would have temporarily ameliorated some aspects of the loss and granted a material connection to their previous life.

KEYES FERRY, JEFFERSON COUNTY, WEST VIRGINIA

The "raging waters" hit Keyes Ferry with a fury that unexpectedly swept away the historic Gershon Keyes house. According to the *Daily Dispatch*, the "old mansion" had "withstood storm and tempest for over a century," making the house a local landmark.[221]

The owners at the time, John Thomas (twenty-nine) and Annie (twenty-four) Allstadt, along with their two-year-old daughter, Mattie, barely escaped before "the house, stabling, farming implements, &c., became common food for the raging waters."[222] Annie Allstadt's father, John G. Cockrell, was staying at or visiting this location during the flood.

Cockrell was in possession of $4,000 in physical bonds at the time of the flood. Likely because of the rain, he "spread them out on a table to dry."[223] However, when the flood struck, everything happened in such a whirl that the bonds were left on the table and washed away with the house. Part of the bonds may have belonged to James T. Reed of Harpers Ferry. When the *Spirit of Jefferson* mentioned Reed's heroism, it also noted that he suffered greatly from the flood, losing "important papers" that were "in the possession of Mr. John G. Cockrell."[224] It seems quite plausible that Reed and Cockrell conducted some business, and when Cockrell made the approximately five-mile ride back to Keyes Ferry, he was soaked in the process and laid the bills out to dry without any idea that a flood was imminent, which may help to illuminate how Harpers Ferry was caught so off guard.

HARPERS FERRY, JEFFERSON COUNTY, WEST VIRGINIA

Imagine, if you will, someone in the telegraph office at Harpers Ferry receiving a message on Friday, September 30, around 2:00 p.m., that there was terrible flooding in the Shenandoah Valley.[225] The rain was pouring down, as it had been since Wednesday night, but the river was still in its banks. However, "before those rumors could be traced to any reliable source" the Shenandoah River "had actually surrounded, with its angry waves, the houses near the bank."[226] Some claim "the rush of its waters" was so rapid that "it rose six feet in four minutes."[227] The *Wheeling Daily Register* cautioned "though probably an exaggeration," that anecdote "will give you an idea of the deluge by which we were overwhelmed."[228] This rush of water set the scene for tragic death—along with property and economic loss—and heroic rescues by people who put their lives at risk to be on the front lines saving those in need.

A view of Harpers Ferry from Jefferson Rock overlooking the Shenandoah River. *Library of Congress Digital Archives.*

Along Shenandoah Street, thirty-seven-year-old retail merchant James T. Reed was attempting to retrieve a few items from his store. By this point, "there was no time for him to get into the counting room": his desk was submerged, and he could only get to a few papers that were already damaged.[229] Realizing that others were in danger, he left the building, jumped on his horse and started rescuing people from low-lying Shenandoah Street as the water rapidly rose. According to a detailed account in the *Spirit of Jefferson*, he saved Mary Nunnamaker, who was sixty-five at the time, "by snatching her from the door" of her house and placing her in front of himself on the horse.[230] He then lifted her "to the opposite wall of the street, where she was caught by Mr. [Charles] Trail." After Nunnamaker was safe, Reed rode back into the chaos, making several trips to rescue James (thirty-five) and Margaret (twenty-five) Steadman, along with their children Marietta (four) and Cora (ten months); Eliza Beecraft (forty-eight) and her son George (fourteen); and George Neer (thirteen), who was "found clinging to the window of the store room of Reed & Hopwood," along with a few others not listed in the newspaper accounts.[231]

What may have started out as a venture to save papers and goods from his business turned into an intense rescue mission—so much so that it required him to change horses, switching to a "second horse when the first broke down."[232] Instead of attending to his personal economic security, he rescued at least nine people. Reed lost "everything he was interested in on this street" where his business was located, "including the Shenandoah ferry boats, ropes, and fixtures."[233] He also lost "important papers in the possession of Mr. John G. Cockrell," which were likely swept away at Keyes Ferry.[234] While Reed was engaged in rescuing townsfolk, "the swift waters cut him off from returning his store," and he retreated to higher ground.[235]

In the near blink of an eye, most of the houses in what was known as Shenandoah City, located "about a mile above Harpers Ferry," were swept away.[236] There is no official count for the total number of dwellings or lives lost in this vicinity. The devastation was so great that newspapers reduced it to broad strokes: "Every building from Shenandoah City to Halls works is gone, and from Halls Works to the old Shenandoah bridge but a few houses are standing, the whole number destroyed in this vicinity amounting to some forty or fifty."[237] From more detailed accounts, it's known that this area had a "large plaining mill" belonging to Wernwag & Gannon, a mill and large machine shop belonging to Childs, McCeight & Company and twenty dwellings belonging to that firm that were either damaged or swept away by the water.[238] Most tragically, there was a large, seemingly sturdy brick dwelling in which three African American families took refuge.

When the water rose in this area, at least three families left their "humble dwellings" and sought shelter in the large brick structure.[239] Around twenty people, most of whom were family, gathered here for succor. James Bateman (forty-five), his brother Benjamin (forty-one) and Hinton Myers (thirty) all worked on the railroad and lived close to one another.[240] According to the 1860 census, the Batemans and Myers were both free Black families who lived in Bolivar prior to the Civil War.[241] All of their families included young children and infants. Seeing the dangerous floodwaters, they came together to wait out the flood in the safest place available to them. When the foundation gave way, the brick building collapsed and took with it at least eighteen people. Official death records include James and his four children: James (fifteen), Julia (twelve), Emily (nine) and Franny (one and a half); his brother Adam Bateman (forty-three); Benjamin and Elizabeth Bateman (thirty) and their five children: Sarah (twelve), Walter (ten), Malcolm (eight), James (six) and Benjamin (one); Hinton and Mary Myers (thirty) and three of their children: Phillip (six), Hugh (four) and Cora (one). It's unclear if

Nancy Bateman, who was married to James, survived. Her name is not listed on the death records but is referenced in newspapers. In the horrible wake of this tragedy, F. Bateman, brother of James, Benjamin and Adam, reported the deaths of his loved ones. Despite their tragic fate, the Batemans and Myers families were marginalized by the flood coverage. Their story was often either erroneously reported or barely mentioned.

In an early twentieth-century local history of Harpers Ferry, there are only three sentences out of sixteen full pages of 1870 flood coverage that mention the Bateman family, even though eighteen members of the family lost their lives.[242] The 1903 book *The Strange Story of Harper's Ferry* describes the Batemans as "humble, hard-working people" who were "a good deal respected for their industry and unobtrusive manners."[243] The depiction mainly focuses on their work ethic and includes a backhanded compliment, essentially reducing the lives of eighteen people to a generalized labor description and characterizing them as compliant. The succinct nature of the depiction of the families and their plight is eclipsed by the extensive coverage of white flood victims, whose stories received greater detail. This is a fault that lingers, despite extensive attempts at research, as previous marginalization reduces the details known about them.

Near Shenandoah City, the boardinghouse belonging to eighty-one-year-old Nancy Evans was swept away. Most of the residents quickly evacuated ahead of the danger. However, Margaret Carroll (seventy-four), "widow of Eli Carroll" and the former proprietress of the Wager Hotel that catered to the railroad depot, opted not to leave.[244] Her housemates were unable to convince her to come with them, and "they had not time to pick her up forcibly" the water was rising so quickly.[245] Carroll, born in Ireland, was revered for her "kindness of heart and accommodation of spirit" making her "respected and beloved by all."[246] A column devoted to her asserted that since she had "no immediate family, had so oft been a succor to the orphans and a mother to the motherless, there are many to mourn her demise and long cherish her memory."[247]

Moving toward this main section of the city, those living in the lower part of town found themselves in desperate need of rescue by Friday evening. Around 6:00 p.m., the houses of James Anderson and John Greaves were among the first carried away on that horrible evening. Those two families barely escaped their homes "so rapidly did the waters surround them."[248] Cut off, both families took refuge with their neighbors Samuel and Casia Williams. From around 6:00 p.m. on Friday until 4:00 p.m. Saturday, the three families were "imprisoned" in the Williamses' house.[249]

Engraving of the flood at Harpers Ferry. Notice the train crossing the bridge across the Potomac. If you look closely, you can also see all manner of things happening in the water. *From* Harper's Weekly, *October 20, 1870. Scan from original.*

Watching the horrible situation unfold, some in the area began to coordinate rescue efforts using ropes and baskets. Daniel Ames, a forty-eight-year-old merchant, and forty-four-year-old Charles King, who worked at one of the hotels, were both lauded as heroes because of their efforts to rescue people from the lower section of the city and Virginius Island using ropes and baskets.[250] They rescued two or three families Friday night, but the Anderson, Greaves and Williams families would have to wait until the following day.[251]

Around 8:00 p.m. on Friday, a crowd of excited and anxious townspeople "gathered at the foot of the Union Street, in South Bolivar."[252] They watched in helpless agony the macabre fate of four families who were unable to escape Overton's Island before the water rose and carried away "the bridges connecting the island with the main land" which were swept away with "first fierce rush of the water."[253] The gloomy, dark evening partially obscured the scene of chaos and was poetically described in this account:

> *The young moon casts a sickly light on the fearful scene, and the shadows of the clouds that drifted over her face and obscured her feeble beams, added a gloom to the already sufficiently saddening spectacle. The light was not enough to enable us to see distinctly the fearful tragedy, but cries of terror from a man in mortal agony, revealed too truly that a human being was hopelessly struggling in the waves.*[254]

The correspondent for the *Baltimore Gazette* explained that those watching from shore believed the struggle and cries for help belonged to Samuel Hoff (twenty-eight), who lived on Overton's Island near the home of James and Annie Shipe.[255] Hoff's wife "had gone to the mainland." When the water got high enough that he was worried about imminent danger, he attempted "trying to swim ashore" rather than "being carried away with his house." In Joseph Berry's account, Hoff was "carried from his own door by the current, grasped a small tree and appealed for assistance" but was not able to be rescued.[256]

Soon after, a light was briefly "noticed on the porch of the house occupied by Mrs. Overton."[257] Sarah Overton (fifty-eight) lived with her daughter Catherine Mills (thirty-eight) and her grandchildren, Edward Waters (fifteen), John Waters (ten) and Archibald Mills (one).[258] Soon after the light was seen, it was quickly extinguished. Whoever ventured onto the porch at that inopportune moment was swept away, and "a grinding, crashing noise, heard at the same instant, made it certain that the porch was carried away at the moment the person carrying the light set foot on it."[259] Approximately three minutes later, "the house itself was carried away and all its inmates drowned."[260] From the official death records, it appears that Edward and John were not at home and may have escaped this terrible fate.

On the same island, Jeremiah "Jere" Harris (seventy) and his family were actively seeking a more secure place of refuge. Jere, along with his daughter, Janetta (forty-five); granddaughter, Adeline (four); and possibly grandson and apprentice Morgan Brown (twenty-four), sought safety in the large brick house of a Mr. Murphy, fearing their "own house, which was much smaller," may have been more likely "to be destroyed."[261] Harris was a well-known and respected plasterer who lived in Harpers Ferry for over ten years and was part of the free Black community before the Civil War.[262] Their succor at Mr. Murphy's house did not last, as it was soon "overturned and carried away."[263] The Harrises escaped in time but were in search of another place to hide from the flood. In desperation, Harris was "heard to moan piteously and pray."[264] Safety eluded them and soon the island was engulfed. In the span of a few minutes, most structures were swept from the island.[265]

The home of James (twenty-seven) and Annie (twenty-eight) Shipe also met this fate. James survived after a horrible ordeal that involved desperately trying to save himself and his wife, Annie. The correspondent for the *Baltimore Gazette* based his coverage on Shipe's account, from which the paper "gather[ed] many particulars of the disaster."[266] When James Shipe "heard his house crumbling, he stripped himself for swimming" and then seized

Annie and "swam with her to the railroad water tank some twenty yards off."[267] He attempted to grab hold several times, but each time he got close, "he was beaten back by the waves it surged around it."[268] He was able to hold onto Annie until "a wave separated them," and she sank under the water.[269] The current caused him to drift "a long way down the stream, and soon he was rushed under the roof of a covered bridge that had been washed from its position at the upper end of Overton's Island."[270] The force of the water and his body moving along the rafters caused him to be "terribly lacerated by nails and sharp angles of the timbers."[271] After surviving that ordeal, he swam to Virginius Island and caught "the window of Mr. Joseph Young's house."[272] While yelling for help, he realized that the "family had left" and that the house was beginning to crumble. Shipe swam to another house and encountered the same situation. Then he noticed "a tree near Mr. Hood's house" that he was able to climb and gain access to the house, since the family had already fled. Shipe found a way to get on the roof and waited for rescue "until a late hour on Saturday afternoon."[273]

A visitor traveling though the town arrived by train after 8:00 p.m. on Friday and departed around 2:00 a.m. on Saturday. Although he didn't see the destruction with the light of dawn, his brief time in the area provided an additional perspective on the night and the unforgettable sights and sounds:

> *Poor women and children were on the streets who had just escaped a watery grave, and every few minutes a low rumble would be heard, the startling signal that one of their once happy homes had sunk beneath the waters together with all their earthly possessions, or perhaps containing loved kindred and friends, whose dying wails could be heard on the midnight air. At intervals all through the night buildings were being swept away.—At one time we heard four fall in less than five minutes.*[274]

The morning light revealed a scene "truly appalling and entirely beyond description."[275] At least thirty-one lives were lost along with over fifty dwellings, "leaving families destitute of food, clothing or shelter of a roof."[276] On Virginius Island, a sawmill belonging to John Wernwag was washed away, and the large cotton mill belonging to Child and McCreight was heavily damaged.[277]

While economic ruin was on the minds of so many in the town, there was still important rescue work to be done. Around 8:00 a.m. on Saturday, an unidentified African American woman was seen desperately clinging to a tree "near the house of Mrs. Nunnemaker, on Shenandoah street."[278]

Barely keeping her head above water, her entire body below her shoulders was submerged in the debris-filled waters; the "furious current was swaying her back and forth, as it eddied round the tree and the houses near it."[279] Hanging on for very dear life, this woman literally withstood the storm. It took incredible fortitude for her to hold on under these conditions, but luckily twenty-year-old William Gallagher and others came to her aid and helped her back onto solid ground.[280]

Those who were awaiting rescue at the Williams house likely suffered from "dreadful anxiety" and fear. Since six o'clock the night before, they were subjected to constantly hearing the "thunder of the furious river, the noise of other falling buildings, and the shouts of the excited multitude in the town." The constant commotion was so loud that the eyewitness took special care to explain that around daybreak, "the side of the house next the river gave way with a loud crash," but all of the sounds drowned out its destruction. Only "the cries of the women and children, the excited gestures of the male prisoners, made it evident that some catastrophe had occurred." The crashing of that house was an urgent reminder that although they survived the night, the twenty people in the Williams house were terrified, and now that there was daylight, it was time to make the rescue.

With the light of day, Daniel Ames and Charles King resumed their rescues via rope and baskets. The ropes were thrown to those trapped by the floodwaters, and "the baskets with their occupants drawn across with a smaller rope by those on the shore."[281] The intensive rescue of the Williams, Anderson and Greaves families was coordinated "from the houses of Mr. Matthew Quinn."[282] Ames made an extra effort to comfort and reassure these families that they would be safe. For the benefit of all those in peril and awaiting rescue, Daniel Ames "went in the basket on its first trip across to the Williams' house," crossing the "raging gulf" and putting his own life in potential danger to comfort others and demonstrate this method of rescue.[283]

Once he arrived at the imperiled dwelling, he assisted the harrowed people with their escape. If all members of the three households were present at this location, Ames was about to help rescue twenty people whose ages ranged from three months to sixty-five. After that, he remained with the family, "encouraging the women" who were "afraid to venture in the basket"[284] and helping with several of their rescues. He took special care to "secure the children with cords, lest they might tumble out on the passage."[285] He waited until "all were safe" before returning to the main part of the city in a basket. The Williams house ended up being a particularly lucky location to withstand the swift waters. Two trees near the house created a shield from

Harpers Ferry, view of the town and the Potomac Railroad Bridge. John Wernwag could have seen this view of the as he rode the remains of his machine shop down the river. *Library of Congress Digital Archives. Public domain.*

the swift water and much of the debris. Early on, the trees started catching debris and formed a drift similar to the one that the Pettys survived on. The drift helped "to break the force of the current," ultimately saving the house and its occupants "from total destruction."[286]

The Reverend Warren B. Dutton (sixty-seven) and Mary Dutton (forty-seven) were also rescued by baskets on Saturday. The couple lived on Virginius Island in one of the houses known as "brick row."[287] When the river rose, they became "hemmed in so completely as to render escape impossible."[288] As the water rushed around their dwelling, part of the "gable end and portions of the front" of their house collapsed and struck the reverend in the head.[289] Alone at the time, he was "stricken senseless in the passage way" and lay prostrated until Mary found him.[290] She attended to the "cut of considerable length and depth on his forehead," which was bleeding profusely.[291] He was able to stand after receiving "the application of restoratives." However, they were unable to be rescued until late Saturday via ropes around their waists and baskets. The older Presbyterian minister was brought to the home of his brother-in-law the Reverend A.C. Hopkins, where he was still recovering from his injuries at least a week later.[292]

Amid all the rescue efforts, the waters continued to rush and swirl through Harpers Ferry for several hours. Around 10:00 a.m. on Saturday, John Wernwag's machine shop on Virginius Island was swept away with him in it. Wernwag was an accomplished machinist and son of the famous early nineteenth-century bridge builder Louis Wernwag. The *Virginia Free Press* noted that he, John (the son), was "a man of fine mechanical genus, although his excessive modesty has always prevented his talents from being known beyond his own neighborhood."[293] This modest engineer marked his seventy-sixth birthday the morning of the flood by working in his machine shop "until too late to make his escape, and on Saturday morning the building unable longer to withstand the current" was swept from its foundation.[294] After the shop entered the Potomac, it struck an obstacle and "parted in two."[295] The spectators swarming the hillside held their breath with worry. "After sinking for a moment," Wernwag reappeared, rising "to the surface of the water between two joists."[296] From the shore, those watching saw the "the brave old man" emerge from the water and "nimbly climb" onto the wreckage of his former shop.[297] He "seated himself" between the joists and soon got ahold of a "floating window sash" that he placed "upon the joist" to secure it a little more.[298] After settling onto the remains of his shop, he waved "to the crowds which blackened the surrounding hills."[299] However, the spectators were unable to do anything to initiate his rescue as he rapidly drifted down the river.[300] A few minutes into his journey, he was lost to sight among the waves of the "Bullring"—the rockiest part of the river bed—and presumed lost.[301]

BRUNSWICK (BERLIN), MARYLAND

Six miles below Harpers Ferry, at Berlin, Maryland, around eleven o'clock on Saturday morning, "a raft of some kind" passed the town.[302] When a man was seen "making signals for help," three men obtained a boat and went after him.[303] It took only around ten minutes for Theophilus. B. Laypole, George W. Ridenbaugh and William Ray to reach the splintered wreckage, successfully rescue the old man and get him to shore.[304] Once they were on dry land, he "prove[d] to be old Mr. (John) Wernway [*sic*], the great machinist and bridge builder of Harper's Ferry"[305] About two hours after he was last seen in Harpers Ferry, "trains brought news that he had been rescued at Berlin."[306] Later in the evening, the "Winchester accommodation train"

The village of Brunswick, Maryland, circa 1862. Here the residents boated through the streets of town during the flood. This less rocky section of the river may have helped John Wernwag to be successfully rescued. *Library of Congress Digital Archives. Public domain.*

arrived with "the old man himself, safe and sound, except a few scratches on the hands and suffering somewhat from exhaustion."[307]

The other accounts from Berlin are limited. A short article about "The Flood in Berlin" revealed that residents were "boating through the streets and flats of their village."[308] For miles above and below the town, the Chesapeake and Ohio Canal merged with the river to become one massive waterway.[309] Although there was damage to local buildings and the canal, most of the loss was agricultural. Corn along the bottomland was completely destroyed just as it was ready for harvest.[310] Berlin, now modern-day Brunswick, Maryland, did not suffer like Harpers Ferry. There were no casualties in this location, and the overall damage was minor when compared to the neighboring city.

From Brunswick, Maryland, to Georgetown, the Potomac River meandered through mainly rural farmland. A letter from Leesburg mentioned heavy rain that lasted for two days, saturating "the ground completely, but did very little damage away from the Potomac."[311] Mason Island and Harrison Island in Montgomery County, Maryland, both used for agriculture, lost a significant amount of corn, with a letter from Leesburg estimating that about three thousand bushels of corn were destroyed on Mason Island.[312] Aside from agricultural loss, the Chesapeake and Ohio Canal was heavily damaged along this trek, with at least several breaks near "Eight-mile level" and one at Great Falls.[313] In order to fix the damage as quickly as possible, the canal company employed about one thousand men and two hundred horses and carts to work "night and day on the repairs."[314]

GEORGETOWN AND WASHINGTON, D.C.

As the flood continued its treacherous path toward Georgetown, Washington, D.C., and Alexandria, the cities along the Potomac were unaware of the impending deluge. The rain fell off and on for three days but was not heavy enough to cause concern about a flood, especially since there was no communication to indicate a threat from upriver. According to the *Alexandria Gazette*, "The people were about felicitating themselves that the storm had passed without inflicting any damage upon them."[315] The lack of communication was an accidental but understandable oversight considering the circumstances. Years before the invention of the telegraph, Harpers Ferry used to send pony expresses to Georgetown to alert that a flood was impending.[316] That practice ended with the invention of the telegraph, but in the chaos, "a great oversight was committed" when that protocol was overlooked, a mistake that was mentioned several times in the *Washington Evening Star*.[317]

As a result, those along the river were caught off guard during the early morning of Saturday, October 1, when the Potomac River started to rise rapidly. The Washington, D.C. *Evening Star*'s newspaper coverage indicates that folks in this area knew about the flood in Richmond and Lynchburg but were completely unaware of the destruction at Harpers Ferry now heading their way. As the Potomac morphed into a raging, debris-filled river, the city woke to find a freshet on its doorstep.

About three and a half miles north of Georgetown is one of the oldest consistently used Potomac River crossings. The Chain Bridge, first constructed in 1797, has consistently been a major travel route in and out of D.C. Named for three of its early nineteenth-century chain suspension bridge iterations in use from about 1808 to 1852, the version lost during the flood was the sixth, a wooden crossbeam truss bridge completed before the Civil War. During the early hours of Saturday, October 1, the swift water and debris caused the bridge to break apart. According to the *Evening Star*, two men who were crossing it at that early hour were "carried away" and "have not been seen since."[318] Several of the large spans of the Chain Bridge floated down the river, four of which eventually lodged against the Long Bridge, contributing greatly to the damage there.

A little south of the Chain Bridge, near the Chesapeake and Ohio Canal, in the vicinity of Edes' Mill, F. Moody looked in on his livestock, which he planned to take to market in the morning. Finding them all safe on the lowlands of his farm, he retired to bed around 1:00 a.m. Within a few hours, the river rose with such force that the entirety of his flock was carried off before he awoke. The *Evening Star* estimated that he lost 270 sheep and 6 cows by around 3:00 a.m., their lifeless bodies adding to the debris filled waters, becoming another morbid ingredient of this turbid concoction.[319]

Without knowing the flood was on the way, those who made their living along the wharves lost heavily. That morning, people hurriedly worked in teams "removing barrels, bags of guano, and all light goods within reach

Overhead view of the Chain Bridge, circa 1865. This incarnation was destroyed by the 1870 flood. Notice the height of the bridge and how high the water must have been to smash it to bits. *Library of Congress Digital Archives. Public domain.*

Georgetown waterfront, view from Mason's Island, circa 1865. *Library of Congress Digital Archives. Public domain.*

of the water."[320] The *Evening Star* speculated that thousands in goods "might have been saved" if the dock workers had received a warning and were able to prepare.[321] However, even with preparations, some damage would have been unavoidable, including that to boats, wharves and structures close to the water. Marbury's Wharf was swept away around 11:00 a.m., and a Mr. Pasano lost "fifteen pleasure boats," nine of which were later found "at different points in the lower Potomac uninjured, and brought back."[322] Approximately fifty or sixty "other private boats" were swept away, including several fishermen's boats between the Chain Bridge and Georgetown.[323]

At the time, Georgetown and Washington were separate cities and would not officially merge until July 1871.[324] Georgetown was a bustling commercial hub with wharves and access to the Chesapeake and Ohio Canal. The Aqueduct Bridge that crossed the Potomac River between Georgetown and Rosslyn was specifically built to connect the Chesapeake and Ohio Canal to the Alexandria Canal. By 1870, the water-filled Aqueduct Bridge had a highway section in addition to its original purpose of carrying canalboats across the Potomac.

During the flood, "an immense quantity of debris wedged beneath one of the piers" and created a large drift. By Saturday afternoon, when the water was no longer rising rapidly, "the upright hand of a child" was noticed sticking out of the rubbish pile that washed along the Aqueduct Bridge. The *Evening Star* explained that with "great anxiety to recover the body," folks rushed to try to reach the child. However, in their haste, several people climbed on the wedged drift, which caused it to shift and break apart. When the drift succumbed to the water, "the body of the unfortunate little innocent sank and disappeared, being carried away by the torrent."[325] In the midst of all of the heartbreaking stories, a bright spot is knowing that many people were willing to risk their lives to come to the aid of others.

The drift was part of an immense quantity and variety of debris that filled the river. One writer drew attention to all of the produce floating by, commenting that the river was "dotted with yellow pumpkins and cabbages among other things."[326] This statement draws attention to all of the farmland along the Shenandoah and Potomac that was devastated by the floodwaters carrying off the literal fruits of the farmers' labors. If you were to gaze across the Potomac that day, your eyes would be met with unimaginable piles of rubbish essentially clogging the river, clots in the arterial waterway. The *Evening Star* reported:

> *Several bureaus, a piano, tables, chairs, washstands, barrels, tubs, beehives, buckets, sofas, desks, carriages, mangled bodies of sheep and swine, mowing machines, ladders, staircases, mill gearing, washboards, stove pipes, doors, window sash, brooms, blinds, bedsteads, cradles, picture frames, benches and hundreds of other things, are all wedged pell-mell with the driftwood.*[327]

With all the valuable debris, the "wreckers [were] having a harvest." In 1870, the term *wrecking* referred to salvaging items from the water, like a shipwreck. In this instance, the wreckers were "engaged in catching timber and such articles of value as pass down."[328] It was sometimes a deadly business: two African American men "catching drift wood [were] reported to have drowned near the Aqueduct Bridge."[329] This may have occurred when several of the boats moored to the docks were in danger. The large boats were lashed together for added security. However, "cords of driftwood and the wrecks of houses" came floating down the river and "lodged against them."[330] This made the services of the wreckers "constantly in demand" for removing the debris before it caused more damage.[331]

The timber salvage became so cutthroat that the bridge authorities who owned the Long Bridge "gave the orders to have the draw" on the Washington side raised to stop the "passage of the wreckers" when they "saw valuable lumber disappearing."[332] Before that, "thousands of men and boys were engaged in carrying away drift wood."[333] The bridge company's action caused "great indignation among the crowd, who contended that the bridge company have no more claim to the property than outside parties."[334] Additionally, those independent parties that "worked all day on Sunday" to gather lumber "complain that…opening the draw" mainly gave advantage to "wreckers owning boats."[335] Although it's unclear how this was resolved, it shows that salvage rights and wrecking was a major issue for some living along major waterways it was at times both needed and resented by other businesses.

While Georgetown was inundated to Twentieth Street, it did not suffer irreparable damage. In this area, warehouses on the water side were completely submerged, and many boats, barges and boating houses were "greatly damaged."[336] The submerged parts of Water Street became filled with boats "plying constantly across the street filled with goods," and "horses

Georgetown waterfront with the Aqueduct Bridge to the right. *Library of Congress Digital Archives. Public domain.*

and teams that attempt[ed] to ford" this area were "almost lost sight of at the lowest points."[337] The *Alexandria Gazette* also reported that Water Street was "filled with floating boats of all descriptions." It elaborated that "boxes, tubs, and barrels"—essentially anything that would float—were used "to carry goods off to places of safety."

Those in Washington were also caught unaware of the pending flood. Some citizens who made their livelihoods along the water no doubt spent their Friday evening engaged in leisure rather than worrying about moving goods to higher ground. Wyman the Wizard was appearing at the Odd Fellows' Hall, and the chance to watch such a famous magician, who was known for giving away prizes to the audience, likely enticed large crowds during his few days in the city.[338] Whether or not those working along the river attended, it was a rude awakening for all.

The rising river caused "the dealers in the fish market" and "the middle portion" to move to other locations.[339] By 2:00 p.m., the water had crossed B Street and "was getting uncomfortably near the Avenue."[340] By that point, four feet of water was in the basement of the Fountain Hotel on the southwest corner of Pennsylvania Avenue and Sixth Street. The cellars between Ninth and Tenth Streets, south of the avenue, were "all flooded."[341] A reporter for the *Evening Star* checked on the scene at Russell's Marble Saloon and painted a vivid picture of the bar at 1:00 p.m.:

> *the water was up to within about a foot of the top of the counters, and a dismal line of bar keepers, oyster openers and thirsty and hungry customers were perched upon the tops of the counters, waiting patiently for the tide to fall. Tumblers, wine glasses, whiskey bottles, golden seal, demijohns, etc., etc., were sailing gaily around the room, on top of the eddying flood, but always just out of reach of the suffering customers on their roost. With them it was literally "Water, water, everywhere, but not a drop to drink."*[342]

An hour later, "the water began to fall with the tide."[343] Most of the damage was along the riverfront. Many of the wharves were submerged and required repairs to the planking. Additionally, goods were damaged, cellars filled with water and the lower parts of the city were drenched, but in comparison to Harpers Ferry and other places along this path of destruction, Washington fared comparatively well.

JACKSON CITY, VIRGINIA

What was once known as Jackson City, near modern-day Arlington, was also inundated. This small community was located near the south end of the Long Bridge near where the Pentagon was built. Ironically, this area was known for being particularly seedy, with lots of gambling and drinking. A reporter for the *Evening Star* visited an establishment known as Job Curnow's hotel and restaurant and vividly described the scene: "On the piazza railing, a row of woebegone-looking old soakers were bending their empty stomachs over, looking at the drift-wood circling around in eddies in front of the door."[344] In addition to the hotel, every house in the area was surrounded by water.[345] The brief article also mentions that the pike road was submerged all the way to Roach's Spring and "boats were running from the bridge to the spring." Little else is known about the flood in this area. Alexandria, the closest city, failed to mention this locality in any of the flood reporting, possibly due to the somewhat transient population and comparatively small size of the locality.

ALEXANDRIA, VIRGINIA

The water's grasp proved to be unescapable for most in its path. Both the *Alexandria Gazette* and the *Evening Star* contain vivid descriptions of the curious debris-filled river, listing out details of the abnormal assemblage. The *Evening Star* marveled at an intact haystack "fifteen to twenty feet high, perfect in form," which was said to have been swept off Analostan Island, later renamed Roosevelt Island in the 1930s. The haystack's peculiar adventure took it across the banks on the Alexandria side. According to the *Evening Star*, it swept "over the river bank by the fishing shore and across the flats, crossed a large cornfield which was submerged, so on over fences and bushes, across the turnpike, and lodged in the middle of the railroad track, where it still stands."[346] The turnpike reference was likely the Washington and Alexandria Turnpike, which became Washington Street in Old Town Alexandria. This offhand story gives a better indication of the water levels along the more rural Alexandria side of the shore. The haystack likely meandered along the agricultural area that existed at the time between Rosslyn and Alexandria before lodging in the area near the Long Bridge.

Here, the raging torrent that began around Staunton dropped all of its ruthlessly acquired loot in smashed, muddy piles along the riverbed. At least four sections of the Chain Bridge were noted as debris that struck the Long Bridge.[347] The water and barrage of debris broke the south draw bridge section to the point where it was necessary to remove it on October 4 so that "steamboats and vessels could access" Georgetown.[348] When the water receded, a tugboat came down from Georgetown to assist with removing "protruding fragments and timbers as could not be reached by the ax."[349]

The quantity of debris pressing against the Long Bridge was so great that there's one story casually noting that it could carefully be walked on in certain locations. The *Evening Star* relayed a tale of a group inspecting the damage to the parallel spans of the Long Bridge:

> *In order to examine this mass of rubbish, the party had to follow down the railroad bridge as far as the south draw, and cross over to the old bridge on a narrow plank which rests on some piles close by the channel, and which are swayed to and fro constantly by the surging water. This is a very dangerous place, as these piles may lift and float away at any moment: but at present it is the only accessible path.[350]*

Damage to the Chain and Long Bridge received drastically different reactions. The Chain Bridge was considered a necessary entity and received

THE BREAK IN THE LONG BRIDGE ACROSS THE POTOMAC AT WASHINGTON.

The Break in the Long Bridge. This image shows how the debris collected on this low-lying bridge. In the distance, the Capitol dome is visible. *Engraving from* Harper's Weekly, *October 20, 1870. Scanned from original.*

The Long Bridge, circa 1865. This image is a good depiction of the two parallel spans that crossed the Potomac River. *Library of Congress Digital Archives. Public domain.*

appropriation from Congress to be rebuilt. It was the only structure damaged by the flood for which congressional funding was approved to cover the cost of repair. Although it took four years to rebuild, due to appropriation and contract delays, when it finally reopened in 1874, the piers of the bridge were raised two feet, a change that evaded future flooding for at least ten years.[351]

The Long Bridge had been acquired by the Potomac Railroad Company from Congress and was in dire need of replacement. The construction style of the Long Bridge was regarded as "unsightly and antiquated."[352] However, there appears to be a legitimate complaint; the bridge's "solid causeway of stone and dirt" was known to disrupt the flow of water and impede "navigation of the Potomac River."[353] Several citizens vocally declared that the bridge contributed to greater flooding in Georgetown due to the impaired flow of the river. However, this known issue was allowed to remain and contributed to another flood in 1881. Writers a few years later noted local aggravation in the wake of the 1881 flood and pointed out that "as the freshet was gradually forgotten the agitation of the matter died out, and the bridge remains as great an obstruction as ever."[354] In this instance, although imminent repercussions were likely, the private owners of the bridge allowed the infrastructure to remain in its precarious state, both susceptible to future damage and potentially liable for future flooding.

From the combined stem of the Shenandoah River in Clarke County to Washington, D.C., the flood made its mark on the land and the people who lived near it, carving out a path of destruction that was reported to be "unprecedented" in areas. However, it is only part of the story. As the Shenandoah and Potomac Rivers raged, the headwaters of the James and parts of the Piedmont also suffered from unusually high waters that wreaked havoc along waterways from Lexington to Richmond.

THE JAMES RIVER AND ITS TRIBUTARIES

Rockbridge County to Richmond, Virginia

Furniture, provisions, clothes, cooking utensils, everything, was abandoned by the frightened people, who betook themselves to the upper stories and expended every energy in the effort to escape. Cries of "murder," "help," "mercy," and piteous prayers and appeals to Heaven for assistance rent the air and mingled with the noise of the storm and swelling waters. Strong men testify that, in all their experience of war and peril, they never experienced such sensations, not looked upon such a scene.
—Richmond Whig, *October 4, 1870*

The campfires of the displaced twinkled on the hills around Richmond, lighting the horizon after ruthless waters engulfed the homes of around two hundred families living along the wharves earlier in the day. As nightfall descended on a city without gas light, one reporter observed, "The utter darkness that reigns is only relieved by the occasional gleam of a policemen's shield."[355] Every member of the police force had been called to duty while the flood raged to "prevent disorder, protect property, or contribute to saving that was in danger."[356] For those who lost everything, did the gleam of a shield make them feel safe? Did the police watch over the personal property saved from modest homes along the river as much as the businesses along Main Street?

Besides an unofficial temporary martial law, the city soaked in darkness and water was forced into an uneasy wait. Those around the campfires worried about what became of their homes and material goods, maybe even where their next meal was coming from. In the city, those who retained the comfort of their houses burned candles and kerosene and possibly worried about their businesses, safety and what the next day would look like. Although Richmond was lucky that a warning from Lynchburg saved the lives of all in this area, so many faced the daunting prospect of rebuilding and uncertainty of what they'd find when the water receded.

THE JAMES RIVER AND its tributaries wreaked havoc from Rockbridge County through Richmond. Tributary rivers, such as the North (Maury), Rivanna and Tye caused immense damage to the southern Shenandoah Valley and Piedmont. This chapter attempts to cover the broad strokes of this area, mainly in the human-interest realm. Although there was an immense amount of damage to mills, farms, crops, bridges, the canal and so on, it's impossible to cover each instance of loss. Like the *Staunton Spectator* pointed out, "From the extent of the calamity a larger portion of the details must go unrecorded."[357]

ROCKBRIDGE COUNTY, VIRGINIA

More is known about the storm and amount of rain in Rockbridge County than other areas because it is the only location that provides multiple rainfall measurements from at least three sources. Near the Rockbridge Baths, John Horn recorded that it rained for forty-eight hours and the fall was eleven and a half inches measured "in a tub."[358] Just fifteen miles south in Lexington, there are two newspaper accounts that place the accumulation at around fourteen to fourteen and a half inches.[359] The *Virginia Gazette* published several measurements taken from the "rain gauge at Washington College" and recorded the final measurement before press at 8:00 a.m. on Friday, September 30, at fourteen inches.[360] It's important to note the vast amount of water saturating this region, because it would affect everything else its path.

The Rockbridge Baths, a community known in the nineteenth century for its resort and healing waters, was damaged by the flood. A blurb in the *Staunton Spector* revealed that the "lower bath house and the kitchen" were swept away.[361] This town also lost a covered bridge that was recently completed by the regionally renowned bridge engineer John Woods.[362] Several of his works were lost in the span of a few hours, including a covered bridge at the mouth of Kerr's Creek judged "to be the best piece of workmanship of the kind in the county."[363] The "neighborhood had strained their means in order to erect" this structure, which lasted less than a day.[364] At this time, bridges were often built by a community, an individual or a corporation for profit (toll bridges) or, in some instances, by the state or federal government. Unfortunately, the community at Kerr's Creek raised funds for a bridge that was completed just before the heavy rain began and was ultimately carried away by the surging creek a few hours later.[365]

The bridge across Hays' Creek was also swept away. Along this waterway, a forge, a dam and several small dwellings succumbed to the freshet. The rushing water trapped several residents before they could escape to higher ground. As their houses soon became unsound, the occupants "climbed trees and remained in them until the water fell."[366] It takes a lot of fortitude to remain in a tree amid pouring rain and rushing water, and some of these families had smaller children. As unimaginable as it sounds, the dire situation prompted several folks to tie their children "to the limbs of the trees and thus held them fast and preserved them from watery graves."[367] It's hard to fathom the terror and trauma small children strapped to a tree with water rushing around them must have felt.

LEXINGTON, VIRGINIA

Moving farther south toward Lexington, the extent of destruction increased at this more populous location. Here, most of the damage described occurred on the industrialized river island of Jordan's Point. The North (now Maury) River "rose with unprecedented rapidity" on Thursday, September 29, overflowing its banks around noon and continuing to rise until around 1:00 a.m. Friday.[368] The citizens of the town tried to assist "those living there in endeavoring to save their property."[369] However, the water was rising so rapidly, at nearly a foot every twenty minutes, "that very little was removed."[370] Due to the rapid rise, several people became trapped in their houses until it was too dangerous for them to attempt an escape. At this point, Virginia Military Institute (VMI) professor Captain John Mercer Brooke "fearlessly breasted the current in rescuing persons and property."[371]

Everyone living on Jordan's Point was successfully rescued. However, the destruction of homes and industrial structures was immense. A letter to Richmond revealed that "a double track covered bridge which was only completed several months ago, was swept away" and struck Alexander's

A view of Lexington circa 1875. *Image used with the permission of the Virginia Military Institute Archives.*

warehouse.[372] This caused both structures to be carried off. Alexander's warehouse was valued at $4,000 and filled with a "large quantity of merchandise, grain, flour, &c., belonging to other parties."[373] Around the same time, several other buildings, including "the toll-house, Patterson's warehouse, the large Confederate stable (now used as a manufactory of fertilizers), and five or six smaller tenements," floated down the river. Another warehouse owned by McNutt & McCorkle was submerged to the second story and contained massive losses in material goods and irreplaceable literature. For some reason, this warehouse contained "a lot of new furniture" and a "very valuable library, containing a number of rare books" belonging to Colonel Harding, a professor of chemistry at VMI.[374] J.R. McNutt, one of the co-owners of the warehouse, also lost his personal dwelling, which was "partially submerged and then turned over on one side."[375] Between two lumberyards, approximately fifty-six thousand feet of lumber was lost. Like other areas along the rivers, so many mills, farms, canal locks, dams and bridges were destroyed that the list would fill pages.

The flood also cut off Lexington's telegraphic communication with the world. As a result, news of the flood in this location took several days to reach Richmond. A letter intended for the Richmond news was sent via horse courier to the town of Goshen in Rockbridge County.[376] The messenger attempted to reach the town by "flanking through the mountains," since it was known that the bridges along the "road from Lexington to Goshen" were destroyed. However, that plan didn't work, and the courier returned to Lexington three days later.[377] Finally, the letter ended up being sent via Lynchburg and reached Richmond on October 7.[378] This story highlights how communication even in larger towns could be delayed if the telegraph lines and or roads/bridges washed out. William Nalle, a twenty-two-year-old cadet at VMI, also wrote a letter to his mother about two weeks after the flood in which he aptly discusses the damage and how the destruction of transportation infrastructure cut off both communication and access to goods:

> *The flood of which I spoke, did a great deal of damage in this part of the country, carrying off some ten or fifteen houses, some dwelling houses some ware houses situated at the canal boat landing near here all the bridges in the river were carried off and the canal running to this place entirely ruined, all the locks being torn up and carried off. It was a rare sight to see large houses, bridges, mills & every sort of lumber go sailing at a rapid rate, down the river. Up to a week or two since, we could get no mails or any thing* [sic] *that had to come from a distance, and it is still very difficult to get provisions. Mails come and go regularly now, as they have fixed ferries for stages &&.* [379]

Since the flood impaired transportation and communication while also destroying many of the warehouses in Lexington, it made goods and provisions hard to obtain. This issue affected those living in the area and was a tangible consequence of the freshet. However, due to the timing, it also produced a specific dilemma for the town. Almost two weeks after the flood struck, Confederate general Robert E. Lee, a resident of Lexington, passed away from the effects of a stroke. When he died, it came to the attention of the town that the undertaker "had no suitable casket on hand."[380] A shipment of metallic caskets had arrived a few days before the flood. However, the warehouse where they were stored was swept away by the torrent. Without a suitable alternative, a search was made along the river with the hope that one of the lost caskets could be recovered.[381] According to Professor A.L. Nelson, a Washington and Lee University faculty member, "A youth reported that he had seen one of the caskets lodged on an island a few miles below the town."[382] The island was located below East Lexington after the first dam. Here, the casket had been "caught in a brush pile" and "lodged in the forks of a tree."[383] Two local cabinetmakers secured the casket and made it suitable for use. This incident, while unusual, helps illustrate the range of influence the flood retained immediately after the waters abated. Here, a nationally known figure was buried in a casket retrieved from the muddy banks of the river. Even though much of Virginia went into mourning, the plight of locating a casket for a person of this renown may help to illustrate the difficulty of obtaining certain goods after the flood.

BALCONY FALLS, VIRGINIA

The swollen waters of the North River met the James River at Balcony Falls, in the area that is near the town of Glasgow. When the flood arrived here, the North River was much higher than the James and "backed the latter stream for two and a half miles."[384] As a result, the peninsula at the confluence was badly flooded. An elevated towpath for the canal briefly acted as a dam, holding back the torrent before bursting. Then "the vast flood suddenly rushed upon the little village of a dozen or more houses and bore them away upon its irresistible current."[385]

The *Richmond Whig* provides a little more detail: "The Residence of Mr. Charles H. Locker, the hotel, post office, lock-keeper's house, and a store house at Balcony Falls was washed away."[386] When the "water started rapidly rising around the buildings" and the residents understood their impending peril, they waded out into the torrent and sought higher ground. From the *Staunton Spectator*:

> *With the greatest difficulty they reached a place of safety, passing through a torrent requiring them to lock arms to prevent washing away. Messers. Campbells lost their entire store and stock of goods. Mr. Jas. Campbell saved only three blankets in which a sick son was wrapped and borne through the midnight flood. Locker lost dwelling, store, everything except the Mill at his Cement works. His kilns of solid granite were swept away. Fourteen houses were washed off.*[387]

Locking arms provided safety in numbers to fight through the torrent and help members of the community reach higher ground. It appears that it worked and that there were no casualties in this area. It's unclear if this flood prompted the community to rebuild farther away from the river.

LYNCHBURG, VIRGINIA

In 1870, Lynchburg was Virginia's sixth-largest city, with a population of 6,825 people.[388] It was experiencing a boom in industry and was a hub of trade with access to the canal and the junction of three railroads. It was the location of the terminus of the Southside Railroad; a junction for the Orange and Alexandria, which ran through the Piedmont to Charlottesville and up to Washington, D.C.; and the Virginia and Tennessee, which ran to Bristol. With all of these factors, it was a city set to grow.

On a particularly dark evening, with rain pelting the city, the brunt of the flooding hit Lynchburg between ten and eleven o'clock on Thursday, September 29. Amid the erupting chaos, someone took the time to send a telegram to the *Richmond Dispatch*.[389] The short message described the beginning of the destruction. By that point, the river was already "higher than ever before known," and it was "still raining heavily."[390] The James River and the canal overflowed. Boats started rising to the height of the canal towpath, and "everything in the vicinity of the canal and the river along the front on the city [was] submerged."[391]

As the river rose, around 10:00 p.m. the "gas-works were flooded."[392] Soon the "main gas pipe supplying the city" was swept away.[393] In the pitch black of night, "hundreds of people collected to witness through the intense darkness the rise of the angry waters and render such assistance as might be necessary."[394] By 10:30 p.m., the toll bridge connecting Lynchburg and Amherst, which was about five hundred yards long, "gave away with a crash."[395] Dramatically, another account recalled,

> the torrent surged and swept around the piers of the immense wagon-bridge across the river, thundering against the walls, swept it away with a terrific crash, carrying the broken fragments, like an avalanche, down the river. It disappeared in the darkness, but was hurled against the new iron bridge of the Southside railroad, carrying it off also.[396]

The Southside Railroad's new iron bridges spanned "both prongs of the river at the island."[397] As the water rose and the bridges were swept away, "the railroad employees at the Southside Island [were] cut off."[398] There are several river islands that were occupied at the time of the flood; although this one was called Southside Island in the newspaper account, the island in question is Percival's Island, which remained a railroad hub into the twentieth century and is now a park.

Returning to the city limits, the residents rushed to save the canalboats that were in jeopardy. As the "waters thundered down the bank of the canal," people actively worked to secure the "packet, lumber, and freight boats" to land using "strong cables attached to such supports that were in reach."[399] Onlookers gathered along the wharves, and through the darkness the "light from a hundred lanterns flashed fitfully across the turbid flood."[400] Those illuminating the darkness in the lower part of the city, still being pelted by

This is likely the earliest image of Lynchburg. Taken in the 1850s, it depicts the massive toll bridge that was swept away by the 1870 flood. Behind the bridge is Percival's Island. *Image used with the permission of the Valentine Museum in Richmond, Virginia.*

rain, also became panicked as worry began to rise that the "ground beneath their feet was unsafe, and likely to be undermined and inundated at any moment."[401] In truth, this was a valid concern, but the ground in the area held. Unfortunately, there were others in the city who weren't so lucky.

Around 10:30 p.m., a telegram was sent to Richmond, warning that a flood was imminent. The last two lines are important because things changed within the next few minutes. It read, "No casualties are yet reported. Be prepared at your city for freshet."[402] This timing of this message is very important. The telegraph lines would soon be down, and this warning saved all lives in Richmond. It also illustrates that the worst of the tragedies had not hit Lynchburg or that they had just happened and were unknown to the writer.

The area around Deane's Foundry, just below the city, was about to be a scene of heartbreak. At the time, the area was referred to as Sandy Hook. Although there are no maps that denote the exact location, it appears to have been an island created by the canal and situated toward the eastern end of Percival's Island. According to the *Richmond Whig*, "The sudden rise of waters" caught the people off guard, and by the time they were aware, "the whole place was submerged."[403] All those who were able escaped across the canal. However, there were several others still trapped in this area. Seeking the highest elevations possible, some were able to make it onto the roofs of Deane's Foundry, while a few others gathered on a canal bridge embankment.

Hoping that they had reached safety, ten or eleven people clustered together on the embankment. In the darkness, Elvira Ransom (age twenty-nine); her daughter, Lizzie (thirteen); servant Martha Ward (twelve); an unidentified African American woman and her three children; and at least three children of Robert Whitlow all waited together for a boat to rescue them.[404] The boat was in sight when a section of one of the southside railroad bridges from Percival's Island hit the embankment, causing it to sink into the water. Grimly, the *Lynchburg News* reported that their "frantic shrieks" were "heard far above the den of the angry roaring of the flood."[405] One of the Whitlow children, likely Cary, then eighteen, was able to swim to safety. However, the rest perished when "the surging waves washed over them forever."[406]

The information about those who were on the bridge embankment is often vague and written with a patriarchal bias. Since the bridge was a temporary refuge for women, children and people of color, the newspaper rarely referred to them by their names but rather how they related to men. Mrs. Ransom was either mentioned with reference to her husband or father. The Whitlow children were often associated with their deceased father, with the exception of later mentioning that Willie Whitlow (thirteen) was among the deceased, and the African American woman and her children were unnamed. However, the *Lynchburg News* gives a hint about their identity by including that her husband worked at Heald's Bark Company.[407] In the census pages near the Ransom and Whitlow families, Sam Bucker is listed with the occupation of "shaving bark." His wife, Eliza (twenty-four), and their three children, John (eight), Samuel (six) and Mary (one), may have been the unidentified family on the bridge.[408] Additionally, the name of the domestic servant with the Ransom family is never revealed in the newspaper. However, the census revealed that she was a twelve-year-old African American girl named Martha Ward. Attempting to restore these identities to the historic record is important, as they were once marginalized by the societal values of the time.

In the same area as the canal embankment, several people made it onto the roof of Deane's Foundry, including the owner, Frank B. Deane Jr. The others were not listed by name, but a report in the *Lynchburg News* noted that those on the roof included several African American persons.[409] The superintendent of the foundry, John Henry, secured a boat and rescued those from the top of the building during the night despite the low visibility and treacherous waters. He "succeeded in landing them all safely" on higher ground."[410] It's unclear if it was his boat that was coming to the rescue of those on the embankment.

Those who were saved from the roof of Deane's Foundry were particularly lucky, both because they were successfully rescued and they didn't have to spend the night in constant peril. Several others found succor in trees and roofs just above the raging water but were bound to those locations until help could arrive the next day. In the vicinity of the "boatyard in the upper basin," two of the workmen at the dry dock, Mr. Wilkerson and Mr. Henderson, were forced into a tree when the area around them became "entirely submerged."[411] The *Lynchburg News* reported that the water was "within a few feet of them" and there was "no chance for them to climb higher."[412] The foot of one of the men was "badly mashed by floating houses which stuck the tree."[413] These people managed to cling to a tree, in the rain, just a few feet above water, with multiple houses crashing into them and mashing a foot. This took place in the city, where people knew that they were there but were unable to reach them. In the morning, they were rescued by Tobe Royalty in a boat.[414]

Royalty, along with his brother Edward and James Moore, seemingly went on a rescue spree throughout the day. Once Wilkerson and Henderson were safe, they came to the aid of Mr. Smith and his family, "who lived at the house just above the new pump house."[415] It was "nearly underwater," "undermined" and almost "turned over." They likely spent the night in constant fear of the house being swept away or bashed to pieces by other debris in the river. After they were safely on dry ground, the Royalty brothers and Moore took off again to rescue those who spent the night in Dabney's Foundry. Here, they rescued "Messers. Percival, Taylor, Dabney and others."[416] Next, they learned that several people were trapped "on top of the South Side Depot" on Percival's Island. Here they successfully rescued E.A. Goodwin, who was the "master of Transportation of the South Side," along with eight others.[417] With just the known names and figures, these three spent the day rescuing at least seventeen people.

The Rolling Mills, located about four miles above Lynchburg, was the home to several hundred people employed by Andrew Wyman and John F. Wood.[418] Those living on the island were caught unaware that "the island on which the work and houses of the operators were located would be inundated.[419] Around 10:00 p.m., the water started encroaching on the low, flat ground.[420] Sometime between 10:30 p.m. and 11:00 p.m., an alarm was sounded, and the residents began working to move the women, children and "particles of value" to the other side of the channel.[421] At this point, the water was rising quickly and making movement "difficult and precarious."[422]

Around 11:00 p.m., the canal "rose more than a foot and several heavy boats and mud machines" were thrown against the bridge, instantly breaking it and "severing communication."[423] With their escape cut off, those still on the island hurried though the water and "took refuge in their homes."[424] The terrified people made loud pleas for "relief" and "succor."[425] One account vividly described the scene:

Cries of "murder," "help," "mercy," and piteous prayers and appeals to Heaven for assistance rent the air and mingled with the noise of the storm and swelling waters. Strong men testify that, in all their experience of war and peril, they never experienced such sensations, not looked upon such a scene.[426]

Boats were launched from the "Southern Bank on the canal to rescue the people left in the houses."[427] All were successfully rescued from the seven large houses on the island. However, about thirty people remained on the island "in the upper stories of their cabins, some in the tops of trees, and several in the narrow strips of sand, from which they expected the waters to wash them away at any moment."[428] From the accounts, it appears that all fortunately escaped death and lived to see another day while also working together to do all in their "power to effect the safe removal of the distressed families."[429]

When the waters receded, the seven houses on the island were completely ruined. What were described as such neat "thrifty and happy homes" on Thursday were now the "scene of wreck and desolation."[430] The dwellings were heavily damaged, "but none of them were washed away."[431] The *Richmond Whig* provides a good description of how the houses looked after being soaked by the floodwaters:

In some of the rooms the broken and scattered furniture remained untouched as the flood had left it; the mud lying three inches deep on the top of handsome carpets, and defiling books, pictures, clothing, &c., all in utter confusion; while from others the fragments have been removed, the beds and apparel stained and torn, the furniture shattered and all piled up in front on the sand, a melancholy picture of family ruin. Around the doors of their houses were groups of the forlorn and suffering people; the women draggled in dirt, and presenting a pitiable appearance. Many of them were actually in need of food; their provisions having been lost, and all but two stoves washed away from the settlement.[432]

Additionally, what were once well-kept, beautiful gardens were now a "wide expanse of sand, dotted with the fragments of trees and planks and general debris and interspersed with steams of ringing water."[433]

A house adjoining the mill, occupied by many of the African American employees, was swept away.[434] Many people living in the house escaped with only the clothes on their backs.[435] In addition to the housing damaged at the rolling mills, the pattern house was lost, and it would take months to replace. The *Lynchburg Daily Dispatch* estimated that the company lost around $25,000.[436] When calls for relief happened in the city, the rolling mills was mentioned as a place desperately in need.

NORWOOD, NELSON COUNTY, VIRGINIA

The town of Norwood in Nelson County was heavily damaged because of its topography, its location at the confluence of the Tye and James Rivers and the timing of the flood. Most of the information about the flood in this area comes from three letters reprinted in the *Richmond Whig*. From the extant documentation, it appears that Norwood suffered the most in Nelson County. An especially detailed account of the damage to the town was penned by "E.W." on October 4 under the title "The Great Flood: Letter from Nelson County."[437] A lot of the information relayed below originates from their narrative, with details augmented from other sources.

During the later hours of Thursday, September 29, the residents of Norwood were suddenly awakened after river rose ten feet in two hours. By 11:00 p.m. the rushing water had started to invade the dwellings and buildings closest to the river. Those living in this area immediately left their homes, "in haste," and waded out in chest-deep water with only the clothes they were wearing when awakened.[438] Despite the rain, flood and darkness, all those living close to the river escaped with their lives and took refuge at the houses of their neighbors who lived on the hills above town.[439] By 7:00 a.m., the river had risen twenty feet, covering the levees on the James and washing them away. The intense destruction immediately commenced after the levees were gone.[440]

First, Andrew C. Stratton's storehouse, post office and counting room were carried away with all of the pending mail bags, letters, goods and stores.

Next, the "substantial T dwelling" of James Matthews quickly followed Stratton's offices down the river. According to the 1870 census, Matthews was the postmaster at Norwood, so it makes sense that he lived in proximity to Stratton's complex of buildings.[441] Then, all except two of the Tye River bridge piers gave away, floating rapidly down the river until they hit the Tye River Dam, and the "whole structure hurled over" it. Next, a two-story wooden building with double wings that served as both a home and store for W.J. Woody was swept away, then went Captain Connor's outbuildings and James Roberts' store and two-story dwelling. Finally, Dr. William Horsley's large double storehouse, surrounded by porticos, and his "lumber house on the canal" are the last properties mentioned by name. Although Dr. Horsley had warehouses in this location, from census records it appears that he lived elsewhere in the county.[442]

The scene then shifts to the canal, boats and equipment along the waterway. Here, the canal locks and part of the stone embankment were "torn to pieces."[443] The canal in this area had several infrastructure components, including the dam, stone embankment and towpath bridge. At this location, "canal boats entered the river here to bypass steep bluffs upstream, and were towed for 2 miles from a towpath beside the river, crossing the mouth of the Tye River on a towpath bridge."[444] After the locks failed, a "packet boat, which had been tired to a tree, went down, along with three house boats and two dredging machines."[445] Residents of the town watched with "intense anxiety," since the boats were loaded with people, several of whom were members of the town and referred to as "some of our best citizens."[446] It appears that the town attempted a coordinated rescue effort, and "after hard struggling all of boats, [all] except one and the two dredging machines were manned ashore."[447] The houseboat that they were unable to save drifted fifteen miles downriver. The reference to the packet boat going down may be tied to a story from another article regarding the Woodson family.

At the Tye River canal locks, Captain William Woodson and his family attempted to wait out the flood on their boat, the *Express*.[448] Several boats were "lying here for protection at the locks."[449] Their plan was foiled when the canal "lock-gates gave away" and their boat was "dashed against a tree between that point and Hughes' island."[450] The force of the water smashed the boat to pieces. Woodson swam while grasping his wife and child for a quarter of a mile. When it seemed that they had finally reached succor in the form of a locust tree, Mrs. Woodson and their child "were swept from his grasp and immediately drowned."[451] The full identity of the Woodson family has been hard to decipher, partially because of the itinerant nature of life on

Canalboat on the North (now Maury) River, circa 1875. This image was taken in Lexington, Virginia. *Image used with the permission of the Virginia Military Archives.*

a canalboat. Since the Woodsons likely lived on the boat, traveling up and down the James River from Buchanan to Richmond, it's hard to know where they considered home.[452]

The article notes that several people were saved by "swimming from their houses to trees" or remaining in their homes for "twelve hours or more."[453] The last tragic scene here involves the Tye River Dam. Before daybreak on Friday, "a house went over the dam with persons attached to it crying for aid."[454] A few hours later, after dawn, another house with "men, women and children on board screaming for help" traced that same unfortunate path. It's probable that one of these instances was the family of William and Judy Jones.

Their terribly heartbreaking story was retold in the *Richmond Whig* through a correspondent from Buckingham County. The house of William and Judy Jones, located on the farm of Frederick Mortimer (F.M.) Cabell, was swept away.[455] That night, the Jones family with their two young children and a guest, Miss Wright, were carried down the river when their entire house was lifted from its foundation. The house and its occupants floated down the Tye River until it reached the Tye River Dam, which was located near the confluence of the Tye and James Rivers. Here, the house was smashed to pieces when it hit the stone dam. William and Judy, both in their twenties, drowned in the rushing water.[456] Their two small children, William and James, along with Miss Wright, clung to the floor of the house and were carried down the river another twelve miles to Willow Bank before they were rescued.[457] Mr. Wright (relationship, if any, to Miss Wright unknown), the lock keeper at Willow Bank, "procured a boat and came to their assistance."[458] After a harrowing journey, Miss Wright and the toddlers were safe. However, nothing is known of their lives after the flood. After losing their parents, it's not clear who took in William, age three, and his one-year-old brother, James.[459]

At least "fourteen houses were carried away" from Norwood, along with "six that came floating down the river."[460] As in other locations, the crops along the lowlands were destroyed. A bright spot comes in the mention of the Norwood School, run by William D. Cabell. The high elevation of the school meant that no damage was suffered and that all "the boys are well and safe."[461] In the wake of the destruction, the Norwood School became a safe haven for some destitute members of the town. On October 30, William Cabell wrote to his wife asking for her help in soliciting aid. He asserted that cities "received most of the benefit heretofore arising from the generosity of the North" but that the "real sufferers in the country have received

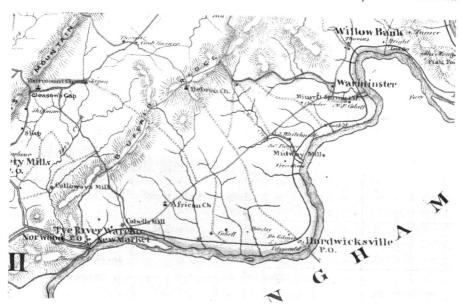

The left corner of the map shows the village of Norwood at the confluence of the Tye and James Rivers. Following the river east to Willow Bank gives a visual representation of how far Miss Wright and the Jones children traveled before being rescued. *Library of Congress Digital Archives. Public domain.*

nothing."[462] This is the only bit of information that sheds light on relief in Nelson County, which was incredibly dire. Cabell ends his plea by noting that he has "75 people to feed every day and many poor people to sustain and not one ear of sound corn."[463]

ROCKFISH GAP, NELSON AND AUGUSTA COUNTY, VIRGINIA

With rampant flooding on the James, the northern end of Nelson County, along with parts of Albemarle and Augusta Counties, was experiencing other problems resulting from the storm. Rail travel across Afton Mountain came to a standstill when the torrential rain caused both flooding and landslides. The eastbound train of the Chesapeake and Ohio Railroad left White Sulphur Springs and passed through Staunton during the storm on Thursday, September 29.[464] Many of the passengers were "returning from the Virginia Springs" and heading at least as far as Gordonsville.[465] The train reached Afton Station but was unable to proceed any farther "on account of a wash on the road and five landslides between Afton and Gordonsville."[466] Instead of being delayed indefinitely on the mountain, the train attempted to return to Staunton.[467] However, after passing through the immense Blue Ridge Tunnel at Rockfish Gap, which had been completed twelve years before by the famous engineer Claudius Crozet, "it became unsafe to proceed any further."[468] The water on the track was so high that it reached "nearly up to the fires in the engine."[469] With both avenues of return cut off, the train stopped on the Waynesboro side of the nearly mile-long tunnel and waited for either side to clear. The *Richmond Daily Dispatch* reported that "between 200 and 300 passengers, many of whom are students going to the University" were detained there.[470] After waiting near the tunnel for about a day, the *Charlottesville Chronicle* reported that the passengers were sent to Mountain Top House for lodging and meals until the track was passable. [471]

SCOTTSVILLE, ALBEMARLE AND FLUVANNA COUNTY, VIRGINIA

Returning to the James River at Scottsville, the water expanded widely out of its banks and covered a large portion of the town. One account claimed that it was "the greatest freshet we have had on [the] James River since the year 1771."[472] According to an eyewitness, the river rose about two feet an hour overnight on Thursday, September 29. The rain had ceased falling by

Blue Ridge Tunnel, Rockfish Gap, Afton Mountain. This nearly mile-long tunnel was engineered by Claudius Crozet and opened in 1858. Two trains got delayed at this location during the flood due to landslides. *Library of Congress Digital Archives. Public domain.*

Friday morning, but the flood had yet to make its full appearance. In a short time, the flat portion of the town from the river to the hill became covered in water. Then, part of the town began to float off. As one account recalled,

To the horror of the spectators, many of the frame buildings were seen gradually rising from the foundations on which they had been resting for fifty years, and move off with the current. At one time six houses were huddled together in the middle of the street, while the poor widows and orphans and others, who, in sweet repose, had occupied some of those buildings a few hours previous, were gazing, with tears streaming from their eyes, upon the awful scene.[473]

Scottsville lost at least twenty buildings that floated down the river and "made their final exit" from the town.[474] This location also suffered greatly in its loss of consumable goods. When a lumber house and mill were submerged, the owner lost about five thousand bushels of wheat. Several other warehouses in this area suffered losses of goods including wheat, corn, guano and lumber. The accounts pertaining to Scottsville are revealed through other newspapers and documents, since its local paper was a victim of the flood.

Scottsville's local newspaper, the *Scottsville Register*, was fully submerged in the "muddy water" and forced to close for several months. The business of cleaning up the shop must have been painstaking. A letter to the *Charlottesville Chronicle* revealed that the owner was left with "a rusty press and fifty cases filled with mud and water."[475] One can imagine the time it took to clean and organize the thousands of individual typesetting characters. When the paper reopened in 1871, it had moved to a new location specifically above the high-water mark.[476] Unfortunately, the damage to this publication was permanent and the paper ceased to operate in 1872.

A letter from Scottsville reprinted in the *Charlottesville Chronicle* also mentioned the losses of several African American businessmen. While specific trades were not described in the letter, the census records reveal that Joe Wyatt was a fifty-two-year-old grocer of multiracial descent.[477] Mr. Wyatt bought his freedom in 1860 for $650. He then left Matthews County and worked on the James River and Kanawha Canal until he saved enough money to "buy property," and by 1865 he owned a store in Scottsville.[478] Andrew Cleveland was a twenty-nine-year-old shoemaker, who, according to the 1870 census, had a "real-estate value" of $200.[479] Washington "Wash" Lewis lost his "new store-house and contents" when they were swept into the canal.[480] A few months earlier, he was listed as a thirty-three-year-old merchant who owned $800 of real estate.[481] The records seem to indicate that there may have been a thriving African American business community in the town of Scottsville.

According to census records, Washington Lewis and Joe Wyatt remained in Scottsville, but Andrew Cleveland had moved his shoemaking business to Lexington by 1880. Although we can follow them based on location, the 1880 census did not ask about personal wealth. So, it's hard to determine how they fared in the post-flood world and what effect the 1877 flood had on their businesses. A few days after the flood, the outlook was bleak. One newspaper correspondent lamented,

> *The calamity of Scottsville is almost complete. Where so recently was heard the merry laugh of merchants, is now heard the complaint, the wailings and cries of her sufferers. Where was seen so recently the busy bustle of her citizens now reigns dejection, irresolution and a general conformity to the gloom and wide spread ruin around....Her foundry, workshop, and mills are closed. Her mechanics and laborers are bereft of the means of support and thrown upon an impoverished public. Our town is almost an impassable firm deposit of mud where the water has receded.*[482]

This correspondent added, "Many millions of dollars cannot repair our damages. Great was the loss here at the close of the war, but never before have we suffered such general impoverishment."[483] For those who lived through the war in this location, this is a weighted statement. General Phillip Sheridan pillaged the town in early March 1865. When his troops arrived on March 6, they "worked until midnight destroying James River Canal, locks, boats with subsistence supplies, and bridges."[484] The next day, they "burned [the] woolen factory with a large quantity of cloth, candle factory with a large amount of candles, lard-oil, etc; large five-story flouring mill, with flour, corn, and wheat; a large manufactory, machine shops, and tobacco warehouses." Due to the pillaging of property that belonged to citizens loyal to the Union, the federal government set up the Southern Claims Commission in 1871.

Joe Wyatt filed a claim for looted goods. According to the claim, "He had a horse and used him on the canal, he also had a little store or grocery in Scottsville in which he kept a few articles for sale" at the time of the raid. In several ways, Wyatt's livelihood was damaged at this time. The canal was destroyed, he lost his horse for future canal work and goods were pillaged from his store. Nine years later, when the opportunity arose, he submitted a claim on May 25, 1874, for $254.62 for "1 horse, 14 barrels of flour, 150 pounds of bacon, 15 pounds of sugar, 50 pairs of shoes and boots, 4 bed blankets, and 2 counterpanes."[485] Wyatt was paid only 138.62 on December 5, 1877, as the agent for his case didn't believe that the shoes and blankets were pillaged from his store. The claim describes him as an "industrious and thrifty man." This is most assuredly an accurate description, as Joe Wyatt had to rebuild his life several times, including in 1870 in the wake of the flood.

RIO MILLS, ALBEMARLE COUNTY, VIRGINIA

About twenty-five miles north of Scottsville, at the little community of Rio Mills, near present-day Charlottesville, the Rivanna River became a torrent of unstoppable force. The Rivanna is a tributary of the James River that passes through Albemarle and Fluvanna Counties. According to the *Charlottesville Chronicle*, "The mill, store-houses, out-houses, dwellings, &c. were all swept away, not a house being left on the premises."[486] One of the millers, Mr. R.T. Jennings, awoke Thursday night, September 29, and "found the water fast taking possession of his home."[487] Immediately, he attempted to save his family. Jennings (thirty-nine) along with his wife, Nancy (thirty-nine), and youngest child, John (two months), attempted to reach the land by wading. Mr. Jennings instructed two of his other children to follow them. The darkness of that night became forever shrouded in mourning for the Jennings family when the events took a tragic turn. According to the *Charlottesville Chronicle*, fear struck, and the children "did not heed the admonition of the father; and after reaching land with his wife and child, he turned only to see his house and children swept onward with the rushing waters."[488]

The Jenningses' neighbors, the Wiltse family, also suffered from a similar tragedy. Here in Rio Mills, three members of the Wiltse family were lost to the freshet. Dolly Wiltse (thirty-one) and two of her children were carried off when the Wiltse homestead was lifted from its foundation and carried down the Rivanna River. Henry Wiltse (thirty-one) and his eldest son were not at home when the flood took place. Wiltse was devastated by the loss of three of his family members and all of his worldly possessions. He lamented that it was "heart rending for me to see my dear wife and little ones perish in my sight, and no mortal hand could save them."[489] While his loss was not covered in many of the newspapers, Wiltse left a detailed account of his plight in the form of a published letter in the *Norfolk Virginian*.[490] It is one of few firsthand accounts written by someone whose house and family were lost to the flood and is an important perspective on both personal loss and the need for aid.

Wiltse's letter confirmed that he was not at home when the flooding occurred. Instead, he was forced to watch from a distance while his house, which was in a low-lying area near the Rivanna River, was surrounded by water and then carried off with his wife and their two small children. His family did not realize the danger in time and became trapped by the rapidly rising water. According to his letter, his house was "the first one surrounded, but it was not the first that went away." The force of the current broke his house "to atoms," and consequently, he "never recovered anything at all."[491]

Heartbroken by the loss of his wife, two children and worldly possessions, Wiltse went through a period of intense grief and emotional distress. His mental state was commented on in the *Rockingham Register* after he visited Harrisonburg during late October 1870. The paper reported that he was seen "wandering listlessly round the streets of Harrisonburg a few days ago, in company with a sympathizing friend."[492] After recounting Wiltse's misfortune, the paper went on to exclaim, "Is it any wonder that [after] such an overwhelming stroke, his reason should totter on its throne? What is the loss of property when compared with this pour [*sic*] man's loss if [*sic*] all his household treasures?—Alas! how little we know of or care for the miseries of others!"[493]

Wiltse acknowledged his extremely distressed mental state and the role that religion played in providing balm for his grief. During this dark hour, he professed, "If I had not asked, and obtained divine help, I would now have been a lunatic."[494] His statement and the *Rockingham Register* article provide a small window into the coping mechanisms and support structures that were available to the flood victims. For Wiltse, support came through religious faith and the assistance of his friends. However, the forms of emotional aid likely varied and are rarely documented in the extant sources.

There are a few other acknowledgements of emotional pain in the aftermath of the flooding. However, most come in the form of brief external observations, and it is generally not reported how those grieving coped with their extreme loss. In the case of Erasmus Kite, his dramatic change in appearance was noted by community members. In the wake of the flood, the eighteen-year-old's hair turned gray and he began to rapidly age.[495] Wiltse's neighbor, Jennings, was reported as being "entirely broken up" over the loss of his children.[496] Finally, the *Lynchburg Virginian* reported concern that James Ransome, who lost his wife and child, was perceived to be in danger of hurting himself.[497] According to the account, "Mr. Ransom gave vent to the most violent and passionate expressions of grief," causing some to believe that he was "in danger of committing some rash act upon himself."[498] Those present then "deemed it proper to put a restraint upon him, and he was taken into custody, to prevent him injuring himself or others during the period of his mental aberration."[499] He must have been released shortly thereafter because the *Lynchburg Daily News* later reported that Ransom went to Richmond to identify and claim the body of his wife, which had been found in Chesterfield County.[500]

All of these statements are brief tidbits that touch on emotional pain and suffering but do not speak to the end resolutions and coping mechanisms available. It is likely that these sufferers relied on friends, family and religion to ease their pain. However, the only extant firsthand source is Wiltse, who, in his time of need, not only depended on his community for clothing and "a little money" but also relied on his religious beliefs, family and friends for emotional support.[501]

GORDONSVILLE, ORANGE COUNTY, VIRGINIA

The Rivanna River's torrent also caused a halt to travel by rail, which was heavily limited for a time with bridges being washed out and damage to tracks. Philena Carkin, a schoolteacher from Massachusetts teaching freedmen in Charlottesville at the time, wrote a detailed account of being stopped in Gordonsville while trying to get to Charlottesville when rail travel stopped in this area because of the landslides, flooding and bridges being swept away. On Thursday, September 29, Carkin was traveling from Washington to Charlottesville.[502] When the train made a scheduled stop in Gordonsville, the usual half hour extended to two hours while "other trains arrived."[503] Finally, they received word that "there was a great flood on the streams ahead of us, and the bridges were either unsafe or entirely swept away."[504] Since there was "nothing to do but make the best of it," those stuck there for the night either sought out the hotel or attempted to make themselves comfortable on the train.[505] Carkin chose to stay on the train and, in very relatable fashion, mentioned that every time "the harassed conductor came into the car he was besieged with questions which he was unable to answer satisfactorily."[506] Human patience for unexpected delays has not changed in 150 years.

Gordonsville was soon "besieged by hungry travelers for food, which it strained their resources to provide" and caused a "terrible onslaught

Portrait of Philena Carken, a schoolteacher from Massachusetts, commissioned by the American Freedmen's Aid Commission. She taught in Charlottesville from 1866–1875. *Carte de visite of Philena Carkin taken by William Roads. Original held in the University of Virginia's Special Collections, accession number 11123.*

upon the poultry yards to appease the appetites of so many hungry people."[507] The train remained there for the night. On Friday afternoon, it moved sixteen miles before stopping at Shadwell, about four miles from Charlottesville."[508] The bridges crossing the Rivanna River and Moores Creek were swept away, stopping the train indefinitely. It's not far from this location that the destruction at Rio Mills was taking place. As Carkin put it, "The Rivanna, usually a tiny stream, which could, at times be crossed in some places on the stones of its bed, was now a raging, seething torrent."[509]

As they could go no farther, it was decided that the train and passengers would return to Washington. Since Carkin was only four miles from her destination, she and a few fellow travelers decided to attempt to make it there by other means. After spending Friday night in Shadwell, she and her companions found an African American man who was willing to take them across the Rivanna River in a boat. At this point, "the river had settled a little, but was still a whirling mass of water."[510] The unidentified man agreed to ferry them over one at a time. Carkin went first, and she noted that when they were "well out in the stream the boat got pretty giddy."[511] They landed in a tobacco field that had been underwater the previous day and walked, leaving tracks of deep, muddy footprints to a nearby house owned by a Mr. Smith. Here, they attempted to secure horses to ride to Charlottesville, but that proved impossible because "there were so many gullies washed out, that traveling on horseback would be impossible."[512] They then decided to walk two and a half miles to Moore's Creek and were accompanied by an African American man, a woman and a boy and girl around twelve or thirteen years old who not only carried their hand baggage but also assisted the party in any necessary way. Carkin could not remember if "these helpers were sent with us by the Smiths" or if one of the party had "engaged the man" to help, but she was very grateful for their assistance, as they "could hardly have gotten along without them."[513]

They didn't make an effort to follow the road, since it was "no better travelling than the fields," and they were "liable to get [their] feet entangled in the telegraph wires" that snaked across the ground with the "poles having been thrown down by the flood."[514] They frequently came upon "ditches of gullies five or six feet wide" and the man accompanying them helped them cross by bringing "a rail from a nearby fence to form a slender bridge which we would cross by clasping hands—the man at the head of the chain and sidle across."[515] Carkin lost count but remembered that this happened several times in their journey. There were other times that they had to climb steep banks by pulling themselves "up by the vines and bushes growing there."[516] One instance even included clinging to a vine of poison ivy, for which she was thankful to not experience the "ill effects from it."[517] Finally reaching Moore's Creek, the "mud be-spattered" group crossed the creek on a ferry that had been constructed. Since their journey had been tougher than expected, Carkin paid for a carriage to take them the rest of the way. This account reveals a lot about privilege and the expectations of a lady traveling in comfort and juxtaposes significantly with the plight of those who lost everything.

COLUMBIA, FLUVANNA, VIRGINIA

The confluence of the Rivanna and James Rivers is a generally placid meeting of waterways near the town of Columbia in Fluvanna County, except in times of extreme flooding, which happens with major storm systems. As with other locations along the flood route, this community was steeped in destruction and tragedy. However, one of its stories, the attempted rescue of an elderly African American ferryman and his wife, was picked up by several newspapers and circulated among numerous southern and conservative papers.[518] Since the Reconstruction era was a time when people were forced to grapple with changing racial relationships, it was not uncommon to see stories that traversed complex racial interactions in the post–Civil War world. During a single decade, the lives of the majority of U.S. residents changed dramatically. Often, these changes were intertwined with complicated emotions, stereotypes, ideals about identity and complex racial relationships.

The span of a few short paragraphs provides a window as to how the predominately white newspaper outlets framed and manipulated a story of tragic death through the lens of racial interaction. The story describes three white men from Fluvanna County who attempted to rescue an African American ferryman and his wife from the ferry house when it became surrounded by water. In the process, the three attempted rescuers died when their boat became compromised. The story, as it was printed in newspapers, actually has two forms, the original full depiction and a shorter tale. The longer story, titled "A Sad Incident," originated in the *Richmond Whig* and was reprinted in the *Baltimore Sun* on October 6, 1870.[519] The *Baltimore Sun* then printed a shortened version on October 7, with the title "A Characteristic Incident." The differences between these two articles reveal certain contemporary attitudes about idealized racial relationships through the eyes of white southerners.

The lengthier article, titled "A Sad Incident," appears to have only been printed within Virginia newspapers and the *Baltimore Sun*. It is more thoroughly detailed and likely geared toward a local audience who may have known or known of the rescuers. This rendition details the attempted rescue of the African American ferryman and his wife by three local white men who met their ultimate demise in the floodwaters. It also mentions the ferryman's refusal to be rescued, claiming,

The house at the ferry, where the James and the Rivanna come together, which has withstood the flood of almost a century, was carried off. The Ferryman—a colored man—and his wife remained in the house until the water rose to the eaves, without any means of escape. For the purpose of rescuing them Mr. Davis, Mr. Fuqua and young Agee procured a boat and went to the house, but the colored persons refused to get in the boat. On returning to the shore the boat was forced by the current against a tree and apart. Young Agee attempted to swim to the shore, and had nearly reached it, when he sank to rise no more. Davis and Fuqua clung to a tree which they had reached, and supposed they were safe as did those that witnessed the same, but the water continued to rise very fast, and it was soon evident that the water would cover the tree or wash it up. The relatives and friends of those men who had risked their lives so heroically to save the lives of the two old negroes in the ferry house witnessed their perilous condition with the most tedious agony. It was proposed to offer a reward to anyone who would venture in a boat to go to the parties. Very soon $2,000 reward was raised for anyone who would go to their rescue. Two of the Messrs. Hodgren subscribing $500 each; but before preparations could be made the tree was torn up by the roots, and these two heroic men and the noble youth Agee (he was but a boy) were swept away by the raging flood. The two negroes remained in the house until it was carried off and have not been heard from since.[520]

This version of the story is particularly compelling because the ferryman was not interested in being saved. The three men, while courageous, attempted a rescue in a rushing torrent of water that ultimately took their lives. It is likely that the ferryman declined their offer for assistance because the ferry house had withstood all other floods during the past century and seemed safer than a small boat on the river. The terminology regarding the ferryman and his wife also changed within the article. When the rescue was attempted, the couple was referred to as "colored." After they declined the rescue, they were referred to as "negroes." The terminology switch denotes annoyance at their noncompliance and derision at their decision.

In contrast, the shorter article, "A Characteristic Incident," was reprinted in Ohio, Pennsylvania, Tennessee, West Virginia and South Carolina.[521] It seems to have been most popular in South Carolina because it was printed in at least three different cities: Columbia, Charleston and Winnsboro.[522] The article lauds and memorializes the three gentlemen who attempted the rescue mission, declaring,

> *Among the many striking incidents of the late flood in Virginia is one related by a Fluvanna County, Virginia, Correspondent of the* Richmond Whig, *of the attempt of the three heroic white citizens of Fluvanna to rescue a colored ferryman and his wife at the ferryhouse, at the junction of the James and Rivanna Rivers. In making the attempt, these three brave men by name Davis, Fuqua and Agee, the latter a youth, lost their noble lives. The incident illustrates not only the self-sacrificing courage of a generous and brave people, but the traditional friendship of Southern whites to the colored race. It is an indication of genuine Southern sentiment in that regard much more reliable than the inventions of the manufacturers of Southern outrages.*[523]

Shortening the article and removing certain details was likely an editorial decision to make the article accessible for reprinting with an agenda of promoting southern white benevolence. The ferryman's refusal to be saved would have undermined the heroic gesture. Additionally, shortening the original article length allowed the author space to insert commentary pertaining to the idealization of southern race relationships. This story from Columbia became a part of the larger flood narrative and helps illustrate patterns of coverage and interest in certain sentiments.

While praising the self-sacrifice and courage of the three men, the wording purposefully bestows those characteristics on all "Southern whites" as racial traits of "a generous and brave people." The title itself reinforces this sentiment with its use of "characteristic" to emphasize the commonplace nature of the act. The article also claims that the act of rescue was carried out due to the "traditional friendship of Southern whites to the colored race." This statement represents an idealized form of race relations in a world where southern whites increasingly found themselves portrayed as discriminatory and racially prejudiced. The article may have been reprinted to reinforce an idealized sentiment often missing in the real world. It may have also served as a counterweight to stories of "Southern outrages." Although there may have been many nuanced reasons for printing this version, this article seems to indicate a white southern need to promote outwardly positive images of racial relationships.

The version of the story that ran in newspapers also eliminates identity, relationships and community dynamics. A thorough examination of the Fluvanna census reveals that the ferryman and his wife were John and Peggie Cary, aged sixty-one and forty-five, respectively. The Carys had four other people living in their household; however, their fates are unclear. The rescue efforts are also more complex than indicated by the article. The "Messrs. Hodgren" were likely Joseph Hodgson (aged sixty-seven) and William Hodgson (aged thirty-nine), both of whom were merchants in Columbia. Joseph Hodgson's household on the 1870 census includes seventeen-year-old Benjamin Agee, whose occupation is "clerk in store." It's overwhelmingly likely that Agee not only lived with the Hodgson family but also worked in Joseph Hodgson's store. The other two people who braved the waters in an insubstantial boat also had associations with the Columbia merchant community. William H. Davis (age forty-seven) was listed as a merchant, and Joseph Fuqua (age thirty-eight) kept the livery stable.

The archives of the Library of Virginia house a broadsheet advertisement from the 1870s in which George P. Hodgson (son of Joseph and Ann Hodgson) and James O. Wakeham (son of William and Catherine Wakeham) were in business together running a general store.[524] William and Catherine Wakeham moved from England to Columbia in 1833 and were active abolitionists. They're known for starting a Catholic church in Columbia. Both of their sons later became priests in the church. It's possible that Columbia contained pockets of nineteenth-century Republican liberalism. In 1835, its population was 177 individuals, of which 30 percent were free Black people. Although that was thirty-five years earlier, the establishment of a sizable free Black community may have influenced the culture of the town.[525] We don't know the motives of Davis, Fuqua and Agee, but it's possible that they were just looking out for their neighbors in a small community and their actions were co-opted for a larger narrative.

RICHMOND, VIRGINIA

On Thursday September 29, the City of Richmond was alerted to the impending flood through telegraph messages from Lynchburg. The warning from Lynchburg gave Richmond approximately twelve hours to prepare for the oncoming flood. The *Richmond Whig* reported that the chief of police called in all officers on and off duty from their beats and homes to "prevent disorder, protect property, or contribute to saving that was in danger."[526] Although there were active efforts to save property, the *Whig* noted that the river "seemed mockingly calm and innocent" and that many residents found it difficult to take the telegraph seriously with calm waters and the sun shining brilliantly.[527] However, there were those who made use of the warning and began moving goods out of warehouses, including Richmond's acting mayor, Mr. J.J. English, who ordered "forty-two members of the chain-gang" to spend several hours "trying to get the tobacco out of Mayo's warehouse."[528]

The *Whig* explained that those working to salvage tobacco from Mayo's warehouse, which was thirty-five feet above the low-water mark, saved 983 hogsheads of leaf tobacco, 347 hogsheads of stems and 100 boxes of tobacco.[529] A hogshead was a wooden barrel filled with cured tobacco that weighed around 1,000 pounds.[530] The chain gang and any others that were involved in the salvage efforts saved over 1,330,000 pounds of tobacco in the hours before the flood arrived. Much of this was for export to the French and German governments.[531] As the Franco-Prussian War was taking place, this tobacco was saved from a flood by forced labor to be shipped around the world for consumption on both sides of a war.

Many of those who lived close to the river prepared for the flood by moving furniture and personal property out of their homes and businesses to higher ground. One engraving from *Frank Leslie's Illustrated Newspaper* depicts people in Rocketts Landing moving furniture out of a house. The advanced warning allowed many of the residents to move their possessions away from potentially threatened areas. However, there was nothing that could be done to save the structures that were fixed in place.

When the flood arrived, it came in with a bang in the form of a five-foot wave. The *Whig* provided a grandiloquent description:

> *There was a sudden and startling sound for the water reinforced by the dreadful torrents from Lynchburg and beyond, poured down with a mad and reckless ferocity that portended destruction, ruin, and devastation to everything perishable that dared impede its conquering progress.*[532]

Manchester side of the James River at Richmond showing the massive tobacco warehouses. The flood warning from Lynchburg gave those in Richmond time to prepare by goods such as tobacco before the waters got too high. In this area over one million pounds of tobacco was saved from Mayo's Warehouse by the chain gang. *Library of Congress Digital Archives. Public domain.*

This engraving depicts a family in the Rocketts Landing area of Richmond removing furniture from their home amid the rising water. *Engraving from* Frank Leslie's Illustrated Magazine, *October 22, 1870. Scan from original.*

According to the *Daily Dispatch*, the floodwaters commenced to "roll down upon us at about noon on Friday" and by "midnight the waters had reached a height unusual even for a freshet."[533] It continued to rise at a rate of "not less than a foot and a half an hour" all through the night.[534] When morning came, the "bright and cloudless" sky made it hard to believe the city was experiencing a severe flood. All those "who dwelt or did business in the lowlands" were filled with dismay by the sweeping waters threatening to engulf their homes and businesses.[535] The river islands were already "overrun with a rapid current," and the bridges over the James were "trembling beneath the blows of the drift-wood and beating waves."[536] As water creeped into the city streets, there was rising concern, but "nobody fully realized the situation" and how the city would be engulfed in the highest water it had faced since the flood of 1771.[537]

As in Washington, D.C., merchants found themselves having to seek higher ground for their wares. Filling Seventeenth Street "almost without a moment's warning" caused the "butchers and hucksters at the Old Market" to get their feet wet.[538] Between 9:30 a.m. and 10:30 a.m., the area around the Police Court and upper part of the market house went from dry pavement to knee-deep water.[539] The merchants and anyone in the area who could lend a hand quickly tried to move goods and stock "out of the way" but were only partially successful. During this effort, Justice William Brown lent a hand: "Barefooted and with his breeches and red flannel drawers rolled up to his knees, he gave his constituents most conclusive evidence that he was not afraid of work."[540] Rather than closing up shop for the day, the butchers made a "retreat to higher ground," and soon the "vendors of vegetables sandwiched themselves between the butchers wherever they could find an opening." The change of makeshift locations and search for higher ground made for a curious sight when "sweet potatoes and cabbages [were] displayed before an undertaker's door."[541]

When Mayo's Bridge, which connected Richmond to Manchester, was rebuilt after the Civil War, the bridge company raised it four feet during construction to better resist flooding. However, with all the debris pelting the crossing, people started watching for its demise. Crowds began to gather on the riverbank, waiting for hours "in the scorching sun" to witness the potential catastrophe.[542] The *Daily Dispatch* reported that some, "if the truth be told, manifested no little impatience and disappointment (such is human nature) that it so long resisted the attack of the element."[543] The river soon filled with all the material goods that it had swiped on its treacherous path beginning in Rockbridge County. The scene is described much the same as it was in Alexandria, with the exception that Richmonders were warned and seemingly treated the flooding more like a spectator sport than a catastrophe. While waiting for the bridge to break, two or three whole roofs of houses passed down the river. On one of them was a "poor half-drowned rat [that] was scampering about wildly, much to the delight of the spectators."[544] Around noon it became evident that the bridge would go, and sure enough, fifteen minutes later, "the part over Manchester creek" gave way and "it was followed in a few minutes" by the rest of the bridge." The police took precautions to ensure that "nobody was on any part of the bridge when it floated off."[545]

After Mayo's Bridge was gone, "all eyes turned toward the Danville bridge, and it hardly seemed possible that it could long withstand the rising current." However, Superintendent Dodamead and his assistants worked diligently to ensure the security of the railroad bridge by knocking "about five feet of weatherboarding" off the "lower part of the bridge," allowing water to pass."[546] They also loaded "a number of coal cars with pig-iron and [ran] them on the bridge" to weight it down. Although the "tide crept up to the very floor of the massive structure and drift-wood was fiercely hurled against it without intermission for hours," it withstood the rage of the waters.[547]

The ruins of Mayo Bridge, circa 1865. This massive bridge was rebuilt after the Civil War but lasted less than five years before being swept away with the 1870 flood. *Library of Congress Digital Archives. Public domain.*

Buildings along the wharf at Rocketts Landing, circa 1865. *Library of Congress Digital Archives. Public domain.*

The low-lying area along the riverfront known as Rocketts Landing "suffered perhaps more than any other part of the city."[548] Once the river rose above the wharves, it "spread itself over whole blocks." Soon, "only the peaks of the roofs of the steamboat sheds were visible." Fairly early on, the James River Steamboat Company's sheds were lost to the waters. Once they lifted from their foundations, they briefly wreaked havoc in the area, "bumping against several houses and knocking down a street lamp" before departing "in pieces." As in so many other places, the people closer to the water retreated to the top floors of their homes, hoping that "the flood would soon subside." When hope was lost, many people were rescued and "carried away in boats to the houses of hospitable neighbors." At least a dozen "small frame dwelling-houses in various parts of Rocketts" were swept away.[549] An older African American man "pointed to his house beyond the dock, which was then nearly under water, and said that he had ten fine hogs drowned there, and that all he had worked for was shut up in his badly used dwelling."[550] In the aftermath, people salvaged what they could, but the floodwaters were often ruthless, destroyers of all in their path. So many people lost all they had worked for, and it's hard to imagine how they rebuilt their lives.

By the time nightfall descended, around "two hundred families" in Rocketts Landing and the lower portion of the city lost their homes.[551] At least twenty houses were entirely swept away, while others were heavily damaged.[552] While waiting for the floodwaters to recede and learn the fate of their dwellings, many families spent the night camped on the hills surrounding the city. The *Alexandria Gazette* reported that the campfires of the homeless lit the horizon.[553] The velvet black sky enveloped the city without streetlights

A person trapped in a house near Rocketts Landing. *Engraving from* Frank Leslie's Illustrated Magazine, *October 22, 1870. Scanned from original.*

or other illumination normally provided by the Gas Works. Earlier that day, the river crept into the Gas Works, and by 5:00 p.m. all of the fires were "extinguished by the flood" and the "engines were entirely submerged."[554] Knowing that the city was about to face a very dark night, the superintendent "notified citizens of the condition of the works," which prompted a "brisk trade to spring up in candles and kerosene."[555] When night fell, some in the lower part of the city turned their attention to "a single gas lamp, that by accident still burns."[556] Although it only cast a faint glow, "barely raising its light in the vast expanse of water," it piqued curiosity and attention because it was only a few inches from being submerged.[557]

Aside from losing bridges and the devastating damage to Rocketts Landing, most of the destruction was physical damage to businesses and goods. The high-water mark was recorded in front of the St. Charles Hotel, today the site of the Main Street Station.[558] For those living in Richmond, the flood was perceived as an unusual and awful occurrence that warranted commemoration. The photographer C.R. Rees marked the occasion with a photograph of Richmonders posed in front of the high water along Main

On Saturday, October 1, 1870, around 1:00 p.m. several residents of Richmond gathered along Main Street near where the current Main Street Station stands to commemorate the high waters of the 1870 flood. This is the only known extant photo taken at the time of the flood. *Image used with the permission of the Virginia Museum of History and Culture.*

Street on Saturday, October 1, before the flood reached its final crest at 6:30 p.m.[559] Those who gathered for the portrait represented a cross-section of Richmond residents, including people of all ages, genders, ethnicities, and socioeconomic statuses. Although it may not have been at the forefront of thought, those assembled in front of the St. Charles Hotel were standing beside a building that less than twenty years earlier hosted slave auctions in the basement.[560] Now, they were posing for the only photo that would be taken of the flood with equality.

As a result of the advance warning, there were no reported deaths in the city, and a lot of personal property was able to be saved. The *Richmond Whig* estimated that property valued at about $1 million was saved before the flood reached the city. Richmonders were quick to acknowledge the help that the telegraphs provided. The *Whig* reaffirmed the sentiment: "When we recall to mind what it might have been but for the warning we received, we ought to be thankful that it is no greater, and the more thankful because it was not accompanied by the loss of a single life."[561]

4

SOLICITING DONATIONS

Relief and the Brief Attempt to Help the Sufferers

The wants of the people are great; in most instances those who need help at all need everything; they are entirely and utterly destitute of household utensils of all kinds, beds and bedding, furniture and clothing. Let no one be deterred from contributing because they have only old articles to give, for we assure you that you can give nothing, no matter how dilapidated and worn, that will not be thankfully received by some poor creature who has lost all.
—Alexandria Gazette, *October 22, 1870*

The children were buried with their mother. The casket had been built so that the little ones could forever rest in her embrace. Their father, Henry Wiltse, survived the flood with nothing but the clothes on his back. When his appeal for aid was published in the *Norfolk Virginian*, it had been almost a month since his life was uprooted by the rushing water that swept away his wife, two small children, house and all material possessions.[562] It was a stroke of luck that his eldest son had been away at school and was spared from the torrent and the scenes of tragedy. They were now the only surviving members of that family. Before the flood, Wiltse lived in Rio Mills, near Charlottesville, Virginia, where he made his living as a miller and had possession of personal property worth approximately $150 prior to the flood.[563] After the torrent took his loved ones and smashed his "house to atoms," he survived off the goodwill of his neighbors and community through the gifts of clothing, food and a little money to help ameliorate his immediate needs.[564]

Unfortunately for flood sufferers like Wiltse, the disaster occurred before the advent of permanent federal aid programs or professionally organized relief groups. It would be another 19 years before the Red Cross began to aid in American disaster relief and 108 years before the Federal Emergency Management Agency (FEMA) came into being. Without flood insurance, social aid programs and official policies for dealing with disasters, it is important to ask how relief came to the victims of the flood and whether there were sufficient efforts to alleviate the suffering of so many people. Additionally, without organized relief groups, who ultimately became responsible for initiating and facilitating charitable works for disaster victims?

While numerous disasters occurred in nineteenth-century America, there is relatively little scholarship devoted to historic disasters and even less on the topic of disaster relief and aid.[565] Since there are no secondary sources pertaining directly to the 1870 flood, examining other events to form a basis for comparison is crucial. The Mill River Flood, which occurred in 1874, is an excellent reference for how relief was handled in smaller industrialized communities. The flood occurred after a dam broke on the Mill River, which resulted in a flash flood affecting communities downriver in western Massachusetts. Elizabeth Sharpe's book *In the Shadow of the Dam* is the authoritative work on this flood and is heavily used as a point of reference. A second example, the Chicago Fire, which occurred October 8–10, 1871, almost exactly one year after the 1870 flood, provides another good source of relief scholarship. This well-known event was massive in the scale of destruction but took place in a localized area of less than a five-mile radius. As such, the relief effort for this disaster was able to focus on a condensed area and distribute aid within the confines of a single city. While the events were different in scope, discussing the fire relief helps provide an additional reference point for understanding certain commonalities of how disasters were dealt with and thought about during the late nineteenth century. Both of these events help us to understand both normal relief practices and unique instances of how relief was handled during the aftermath of the 1870 flood.

The most common source of information about the 1870 flood relief efforts comes from newspaper accounts and letters, wherein representation of voice tends to mainly focus on middle-class or elite white men in positions of social and political power. Flood victims are rarely represented. However, the occasional letter describing their plight was published in newspapers. Examples like Wiltse's story offer a window into the suffering of those whose lives were uprooted because of flood damage. Unfortunately, few of the descriptions originate from the actual survivors. In the case of Henry Wiltse, we learn that he had been left destitute and survived through the help of his neighbors. Since most of the aid that was organized through official channels was not distributed until December 1870 or January 1871, this would appear to be the likely scenario for many in Virginia. Although there is a dearth of first-hand sources and equal representation of voice, this chapter attempts to reveal the plight of the working class and poorer people as they sought aid from the 1870 flood.

Since the flood affected a large area, including several cities, towns and rural locations, relief committees were generally called to order for each county and city in the affected region. Additionally, sympathetic cities such as Norfolk, Virginia; Baltimore, Maryland; and Philadelphia, Pennsylvania. also contributed by establishing organized relief committees to collect donations. On a larger scale, there was a statewide legislative committee in Virginia tasked with distributing funds to the smaller local committees. The abundance of committees and interactions between the multiple entities makes the relief efforts for the disaster somewhat difficult to unravel and follow since there were so many people involved and not all of the committees published their work.

When the "Great Freshet" struck in late September 1870, communities and good neighbors rushed to help alleviate the physical needs of those in distress. The immediate focus was on obtaining food, clothing and material goods. In several cases, people survived with only the clothes on their backs. Since the flood struck numerous areas during the night, many of the flood survivors escaped in varying states of undress. Although the weather was fairly mild at the time of the freshet, cold weather was only a few weeks away, making warm clothing an urgent health necessity. Food was also scarce for those rendered destitute. Many lost their personal stores of food, and without money, they could not purchase provisions. Starvation became a distinct possibility. This particular need was addressed in the one of the first publicized aid plans as a primary concern. A letter from October 4 that was published in the *New York Herald* specifically states, "Starvation stares thousands in the face unless prompt assistance and supplies are furnished."[566] The letter, written by former Confederate general John D. Imboden, goes on to outline a plan for purchasing food for the flood victims and laid the groundwork for organized statewide relief in Virginia. Finally, shelter was a legitimate concern and need, but it was rarely addressed within the context of the local relief committees, likely due to lack of funds and resources.

Although the flood affected parts of Virginia, West Virginia and Maryland, the majority of the damage occurred in western and central Virginia and a small part of the West Virginia panhandle. In West Virginia, Harpers Ferry and South Bolivar are part of Jefferson County and were the only locations outside of Virginia to receive large amounts of aid through a separate local committee. While the damage there was terrible, Jefferson County was the singular focus of relief for West Virginia. In contrast, the affected areas in Virginia were geographically spread out and required massive aid distribution on a statewide scale. Monetary aid and provisions were immediately needed for those who had lost their homes and livelihoods across the region. Compiled information from the affected area indicates that hundreds of families were rendered homeless in Virginia along with "more than fifty" in West Virginia.[567] It is also likely that many jobs were either lost or suspended due to the destruction of industry and infrastructure.

After wading through the wreckage and seeing the plight of people who lived along the rivers in Virginia and West Virginia, relief committees began to pop up locally throughout the region. While several relief groups have been located through research, this part directs its focus toward a few representative examples, specifically the committees in the city of Lynchburg, Page County and the city of Richmond. Each location reveals a different approach to how relief was handled during the aftermath of the 1870 flood. The Virginia Legislative Relief Committee is also examined due to its role as the official statewide body for fund distribution. Explanations of its successes and failures are woven through this narrative. Finally, the citizens' committee in Harpers Ferry is analyzed because it was the only committee formed for West Virginia relief and operated independently of the other committees. The interactions between the various committees and their publication of resolutions are important to understanding how aid was thought about, solicited and distributed within the affected region.

A STATEWIDE RELIEF SOLUTION: THE VIRGINIA LEGISLATIVE RELIEF COMMITTEE

As soon as the extent of the damage was known, appeals for relief began to ring loudly both in the affected region and in areas with close business ties to the vicinity. Virginia's official plan for relief was derived from an appeal published four days after the flood by John D. Imboden, a prominent citizen and businessman from Staunton, Virginia. Imboden publicly appealed for relief in the *New York Herald* on October 4, 1870, in order to help the thousands of people who were potentially facing immediate starvation as a result of the flood. His plan called for one of the larger organizations in New York City to receive donations and then send them directly to the Virginia governor's office. Imboden was in New York at the time of the flood and utilized his business and social connections to draw attention to the disaster.

His public letter outlined a plan of action: "Governor Walker can organize committees of members from the devastated counties, who would at once through their boards of supervisors in the counties be able to distribute the funds properly in the purchase and delivery of flour, meal and salt to the destitute families in their midst."[568] Imboden admitted that the published suggestions were made without consulting the governor. His letter states, "I have had no time to correspond with Governor Walker on this subject, but I know the man and know how well and how energetically and faithfully he will perform this office of charity and philanthropy to a suffering people."[569] Imboden made and acted on these plans from New York after receiving correspondence from his family. Five days later, he wrote to his wife and acknowledged the letter by mentioning that she might have seen it reprinted in the *Richmond Whig*.[570]

Imboden's private letter to his wife does not confess any personal or political gain. From its wording, he seems to have been genuinely concerned with the well-being of the flood sufferers. If there was an ulterior motive, private correspondence to his wife may have been a secure place to vocalize personal ambitions. However, other motivations are absent from his extant correspondence. While professing altruistic motives, it is also possible that he utilized the publicity of the letter as a chance to build personal or political renown.

This method of public charity does not necessarily conflict with the wish to alleviate suffering and was common in the mid-nineteenth century. In *Yankee Town, Southern City*, Steven Tripp discusses how the wealthy elites of Lynchburg "orchestrated several grand gestures on behalf of the poor" that "enabled them publicly to exhibit their wealth, power and generosity."[571] The published letter was a masterful public display of generosity that was likely beneficial to Imboden's image, bringing him media coverage in Virginia and along certain areas of the East Coast. It was also cost-effective because it added name recognition without having to contribute actual money. Imboden's dearth of personal donations was never publicly mentioned and is only known because of private correspondence to Governor Walker.[572]

Portrait of John D. Imboden. His letter to the *New York Times* helped initiate fundraising for relief. *Library of Congress Digital Archives. Public domain.*

With regard to potential political maneuvering, it is possible but unlikely that Imboden sought to embarrass Governor Walker's Republican administration. Governor Walker won the gubernatorial election in 1869 with the support of white conservative voters, who regarded him as a moderate for his lobbying work with Congress to support universal suffrage as part of the readmission terms.[573] The 1869 election marked the end of the radical Reconstruction in Virginia. With his support, the Underwood Constitution was passed, and Virginia was readmitted to the Union without test-oath and disenfranchisement clauses.[574] While their official party alignments differed, some scholarship suggests that Walker was a "party man in name only," changing political alliances with prevailing opportunities.[575] At the time of the flood, Walker was fortunate to have a good working relationship with the state legislature. This would start to change in 1871 during debates over the management of Virginia's state debt.[576]

In regards to aid, General Imboden's call to action was swift and served to emphasize the urgency of action on behalf of people who were devastated by one of the worst natural disasters that had occurred in Virginia. His actions were likely fueled by his personal knowledge and connection to the destruction. In a letter to Governor Walker dated October 8, Imboden reveals that his own family had lost a large amount of property in the flood. While forwarding a received donation, he made a point to apologize for being unable to contribute to the very fund he is promoting because his father and brothers lost "about $2000" in crops. As such, he was already obligated "to aid our old parents with all we can share to replace their lost crop."[577] As a person with social connections and personal knowledge of the damage, Imboden was in a prime position to advocate for those who had lost so much. Unfortunately, it took the governor and the Virginia legislature almost a week to respond and organize the formal committee to collect and administer aid.

During this time, many newspapers called on their readers to donate to this cause. A newspaper in Tennessee commented on Virginia's tragedy: "Let us think and act feelingly for those whom an inscrutable Providence has seen fit to so severely chastise."[578] The *Philadelphia Inquirer* printed a message of unity: "'Their sad lot might easily have been ours; The sufferers are really our neighbors, and, in ministering to their wants and relieving their pressing necessities, we will realize the truth of the precept that, 'It is better to give than to receive.'"[579] The emphasis on neighborly actions and signs of goodwill is an important indicator that Reconstruction America was attempting to shed its animosity.

One of the most touching appeals was printed in the *New York Times*. Petitioning readers, the column declared,

> *The Valley of Virginia is ravaged as cruelly as though fire and sword had once more visited it; along the James and the Potomac, there is such distress as has not been since the dark days of the rebellion. A calamity like this should be the means of showing that we know no political differences in the presence of distress. The Quaker's formula of "How much do you sympathize with them?" will suit the present case admirably, and before many days are over, ought to find a response from the wealth and commerce of this State such as will convince Virginia how truly we sympathize with her in this hour of deep misfortune.*[580]

The sincere appeal uses a call for relief in direct correlation to healing battle wounds, utilizing the disaster as a mechanism for putting aside political differences and rebuilding ties between the estranged states. Simple and direct, the argument first calls for using the disaster as an opportunity to rebuild connections. The appeal for sympathy reminds the readers that it could have been them. This sentiment is reinforced by earlier aspects of the article describing the "elemental might" of water and how the "willing servant of man" can unpredictably "become his tyrant."[581] The necessity to openly call for sympathy and forgiveness is an overt reminder that the war was over but it was far from forgotten.

Although appeals for relief were openly declared in newsprint, it took several days for an official plan to be enacted. Six days after the Imboden letter was published in the *New York Herald*, Governor Walker took Imboden's publicized advice and officially called for the Virginia legislature to organize a joint committee to collect and distribute aid. By this point, the governor's office had already received at least $1,600 in donations.[582] With all of the unsolicited publicity, there was likely enough public pressure to ensure a committee would be formed. To fail to do so could initiate a public backlash and the loss of goodwill across the governor's constituency. However, without Imboden's bold move, the fate of the relief efforts would be less certain. Surely, local efforts would have popped up independently, but it seems unlikely that a statewide effort would have been spearheaded. As such, the statewide relief fund was able to capitalize on the sentiments of wealthier philanthropists in the wake of disaster coverage, striking while the iron was hot or at least still warm.

The Virginia Legislative Relief Committee was composed of three senators and five representatives chosen from areas of Virginia most affected by the flood.[583] The choice of committee members was meant to guarantee prompt and fair action. However, it took almost three weeks after the waters abated for an official plan for relief to be finally released by the committee.[584] The plan called for localities around the state to set up relief committees to solicit donations. In areas unaffected by the flood, donations were requested to be submitted to the capital for distribution by the statewide relief committee. The announcement of the official efforts took much longer to organize than the independent groups in Virginia and the relief committee in Harpers Ferry.

When compared to the Chicago Fire and Mill River flood, the coordination of Virginia's official relief plan moved at a snail's pace and was rather disorganized. Within forty-eight hours of the Chicago Fire, a general relief fund had been created by the aldermen of the city.[585] However, the Chicago mayor turned over the official relief actions to the Relief and Aid Society, a private charitable organization, four days after the fire had been extinguished. Similarly, the official Mill River flood relief committee took about four days to organize. Relief efforts there began closer to the style of the Virginia flood. Almost immediately after the flood, local groups sprang up to distribute food and clothing. Active fundraising began two days after the Mill River flood when Governor Thomas Talbot, who had grown up in the western Massachusetts community, gave $200 "to start a relief fund."[586] Shortly after, an organized "valley-wide" relief fund emerged with a committee of appointed representatives, mainly from the wealthiest town.[587] From a timeline perspective, both Chicago and the Mill River Valley were on top of the organizational game when compared to the twenty days it took for the official organization of relief in Virginia.[588]

LYNCHBURG RELIEF

While waiting for an official plan and leadership from the state government, citizens and religious figures across Virginia initiated relief efforts to serve the immediate needs of the sufferers. In Lynchburg, the call for meetings began on September 30.[589] However, it took several weeks and meetings before the official local committee was formed. The situation was so dire that immediate relief came through caring neighbors and clergy who worked to obtain donations of food and clothing during the aftermath. The Rolling Mills area outside of Lynchburg, a working-class, company town community, was in particular distress. According to a letter published in the *Lynchburg Daily News*, "The houses were all flooded, and with one exception, moved from their foundation. Many of the operatives are entirely without money, and the clothing of many was washed away."[590] Reverend C.C. Bitting of Lynchburg's First Baptist Church appealed to the citizens of Lynchburg to give any "useful" clothing and provisions.[591] The newspaper accounts suggest that he diligently worked with the people at Rolling Mills to alleviate their immediate needs. Examining the historical context of Lynchburg's religious institutions reveals how Reverend Bitting was an appropriate figure to undertake this direct relief role.

The First Baptist Church was one of two evangelical churches in Lynchburg that encouraged the wealthy members of their congregations to treat laboring whites as "moral and spiritual equals."[592] The First Baptist congregation fostered an egalitarian environment that voted on church business democratically and rejected class animosity within the bounds of the church. Members were also involved with the creation of one of the first African American churches in Lynchburg, African Baptist Church.[593] Their more egalitarian ideals and ties to the laboring community likely influenced the decision to help the Rolling Mills community. Reverend Bitting's actions were later publicly deemed successful in a follow-up letter to the *Lynchburg Daily News* wherein the residents of Rolling Mills expressed their thanks to the Lynchburg citizens.[594]

In general, the *Lynchburg Daily News* provides excellent insight into the mechanics of forming a local relief committee. Since the *Daily News* was a daily paper, the modern reader gets a play-by-play of calls for meetings and the local politics of alleviating need. Published accounts of relief efforts began with a brief article on September 30 suggesting that the mayor of Lynchburg call a public meeting "to devise some measures for their relief."[595] This was followed on October 3 by the ladies in the city requesting a town meeting to create "systematic organization."[596] Mayor James M. Cobbs acquiesced to this request and called a public meeting on October 4. However, that meeting was postponed until October 5 and received only a small turnout. As a result, the October 6 edition ran an article publicly shaming the town for its lack of enthusiasm for the relief efforts. This article also implored the mayor to call another meeting to let the "citizens of every circle, pursuit, party and faith, meet and exhibit active, practical and prompt sympathy."[597]

Since the official local committee was taking so long to form, the mayor's office became the central location in the city for depositing donations of money, clothing or provisions. It was left for Mayor Cobbs to "place them in proper hands for immediate distribution."[598] While Lynchburg waited for news of the official committee, the mayor and president of the city council called a meeting of ministers from several churches in the city. The meeting took place on October 19 and included clergy from nine Lynchburg churches: Court Street Methodist, St. Francis Catholic, St. Paul's Episcopal, Methodist Protestant Church, Baptist Church, Second Presbyterian, Centenary Church, First Presbyterian and Grace Church.[599] The resulting local committee comprised nine men appointed by the aforementioned congregations in Lynchburg.

Conspicuously missing are the prominent African American congregations. Lynchburg did not include Court Street Baptist, African Baptist and Colored Methodist Church in the committee. It is possible that by choosing predominantly white congregations, the elite community was exerting and reinforcing a measure of control over the Black community, whose first source of independence had been through taking control of religious organizations. One of the first African American celebrations of freedom in post–Civil War Lynchburg took place in June 1866 as a parade to commemorate the "first anniversary of the first Black-run Sunday schools."[600] According to Tripp, the parade included 1,500 African Americans accompanied by musicians "march[ing] down Lynchburg's main streets, most carrying banners with political, religious, and moral messages."[601] During the postwar years, the Black community grew in autonomy, and by 1870, several social and volunteer organizations existed.[602] Tripp noted that these included "a debating club, a temperance society, a women's social circle and several fraternal organizations."[603] Since organizations like this often provided "emotional support, financial assistance, a common identity, and opportunities for advancement in the community," it's possible that the African American community also received relief through social organizations.[604] Although organizing relief through predominately white religious institutions may have been an attempt to reestablish the bonds of paternalism that often governed Lynchburg's charity efforts prior to the war, the Black community may have established its own autonomous mechanisms for community relief. However, if this is the case, it was not covered in the accessible, extant media.

The call for intervention by religious representatives was not uncommon and is frequently intertwined with the 1870 flood relief efforts. The official resolution by the Virginia Legislative Relief Committee appeals to clergy within the state to take up a "collection of contributions to the 'Flood Relief Fund,' and to solicit the active sympathies of their churches in swelling the amounts to as large a sum as the members may feel able to contribute."[605] Religious language is repeatedly used; themes evoking Christian duty and obligation to those in need exist in almost every relief appeal.

Once the Lynchburg relief committee was officially formed, the information about its work became scarce. Similarly, the Virginia Legislative Relief Committee published only three main articles during October 1870, and the amount of overall newspaper coverage regarding relief efforts substantially declines after November 1, 1870. According to Tripp, the *Lynchburg News* reported that the relief organization had raised only "a small amount...for distribution" to the poor.[606] The relief committee determined to "confine the charity to the most destitute—to infirm persons and widows with little children."[607] At this point, Lynchburg's charities were at a crossroads, forcing them to rethink traditional monetary charity. Tripp asserts many of the standing church relief funds were broke and attempting to find new ways to help the poor.[608] The paternalism and personalism that once existed in Lynchburg's charity structure was significantly altered after the war due to "financial constraints and the emergence of a more competitive and impersonal economic structure."[609]

A few newspapers continued to cover the relief distributions sporadically. However, the publication of relief measures in Virginia was hit or miss and the complete opposite of the Chicago Relief and Aid Society. Chicago's published special report included a general mission statement, an act of incorporation, all committee proceedings, donations and distributions.[610] While it was written by the committee and for all intents and purposes included no real oversight, it did make relief numbers available for public scrutiny and reveals that Chicago's relief effort was much more organized and sophisticated than the official measures in Virginia.

The only official publication of donation amounts collected by the Virginia Legislative Relief Committee appeared in newspapers around October 26, 1870. The official "Appeal for Relief" acknowledged five fairly large monetary donations amounting to $3,150.00 total.[611] This sum was in no way sufficient to alleviate the suffering of thousands of people in Virginia. In contrast, the Chicago relief report acknowledged that 14,137 families were receiving aid in the city on November 18, 1871, with a total amount of contributions listed as $3,418,188.20.[612] While the Chicago committee also reported a deficit of $558,310.34, historian Karen Sawislak argues that the committee actually ended its relief efforts with a surplus of monetary donations that it chose not to distribute and returned to the general operating budget.[613] Whether or not the Chicago committee actually had surplus funds, it is apparent that it was much better organized than the Virginia Legislative Relief Committee and deftly managed to elicit sympathy and open wallets.

If the Chicago Aid and Relief Society's reported contributions are divided by the number of families it was serving in November 1871, it appears that the average family could have received approximately $241.79. The society was also paying salary to 643 employees, which removed $9,758.98 from the operating budget on a weekly basis, revealing the extent of organizational capital.[614] By comparison, if a low estimate of at least 300 homeless families in Virginia received the same amount of aid, the state would have needed to raise at least $72,537.

This could have been a feasible task. The Mill River relief fund raised about $93,000 but had an active relief committee that began soliciting donations four days after the disaster. When the official statewide relief committee for Virginia announced a plan of action, it was twenty days after the flood and momentum was falling. Since the Virginia Legislative Committee raised only a reported $3,150.00 during the first month, it became increasingly unlikely that it would come close to being able to procure a large amount of money to aid the 1870 flood victims. In the end, the governor's office received a total of $4,569.27.[615] Although there were some institutions and groups that donated funds and goods directly, it is clear that the relief efforts fell short. If the low estimate of sufferers relied only on the known donations to the statewide relief fund, they would have received on average a minor allotment of approximately $14.93 per family from the Virginia Legislative Relief Committee. In actuality, distributions could be far less, as revealed in Page County, Virginia.

PAGE COUNTY, VIRGINIA: RELIEF DISTRIBUTIONS

Located in the Shenandoah Valley, Page County was one of the hardest-hit locations in the state. Lives, businesses, homes, material possessions and acres of crops were lost. The total number of dwellings destroyed in this area is unclear. The *Page Courier* mentioned by name at least nine families who lost houses in the flood. However, the newspaper also made vague comments: "All houses immediately on the river were either badly damaged or washed away."[616] While the full amount of damage is not known, it is likely that at least thirty-six dwellings were lost in the county.[617] Although there was significant damage to businesses and other sources of livelihood, the relief committee appears to have directed monetary and tangible good donations to those who physically lost their homes, personal material possessions and food stores.

Since the flood was one of the worse natural disasters to hit the area, it was a topic of interest for the local newspaper for several weeks. As a result, the Page County Relief Committee was one of the best in the state for publishing detailed relief accounts of both receipts and distributions on a monthly basis. Although this committee was very active, organized quickly, and reached out to other localities, published accounts reveal that Page County as a whole received only $707.60 in total monetary donations, including $355.91 from the Virginia Legislative Relief Fund by early December 1870.[618] While each person who received a distribution was not listed by name, those who received material goods in the Springfield Township were acknowledged in the newspaper with a full account of donated items. In this location, sixteen households were granted some measure of relief ranging from $5.00 in cash to an assortment of material goods. Out of the sixteen families that received relief in the Springfield area, three were African American.[619] This committee appears to have based relief allotments on size of household and what was lost, with the largest relief allotment going to Noah and Bettie Fleming's family of six.[620]

A little more money was received in December 1870 when Senator John Roller authorized John W. Watson, the chairman of the Page County Relief Committee, to draw half of the funds that Washington J. Jackson of Philadelphia raised with their relief committee.[621] Senator Roller made a "trip North" toward the beginning of November to advocate for funds. As a result, an additional $238 was raised and split equally between Page and Rockingham Counties. The additional $119 brings the known total for Page County to $826.60.

Page County's material donations were given by the Committee of Corn Exchange in Alexandria, Virginia. The committee also provided donations to Warren County "in the form of money, clothing, and furniture" and may have specifically been active in the Shenandoah Valley relief efforts due to economic ties to the region.[622] According to the *Alexandria Gazette*, three representatives of the Corn Exchange Committee visited Front Royal (Warren County), Harrisonburg (Rockingham County), New Market (Shenandoah County) and Luray (Page County) to survey the damage and assess the status of organizing relief in the days following the flood.[623] Although seeing the devastation surely made an impact on their work, meeting with community members and getting a feel for the state of organizing made a large impact on how relief proceeded in these areas. For example, when the committee realized that Front Royal and Harrisonburg were not making an "organized effort" to solicit relief, it suggested that committees be formed to work with the Corn Exchange.[624] In both areas, the cities were receptive to this idea and started relief committees after the Corn Exchange suggestion. Because of geographical travel logistics and being the "most convenient point of distribution" the Corn Exchange also suggested that the Shenandoah Iron Works in Page County be treated as a part of the Rockingham Relief Committee.[625] During the visit that occurred before October 22, the Corn Exchange left $100 with each of the locations to attend to immediate needs.[626]

The visit revealed the extent of desperation and need for those "who lost all." As a result, the committee made a heartfelt plea to the citizens of Alexandria for any donations, "no matter how dilapidated and worn."[627] By October 22, the Committee of the Corn Exchange had raised $1,284, mainly from small donations, each being acknowledged in the *Alexandria Gazette*.[628]

Their efforts to fundraise and collect material goods made a difference for those living in the Shenandoah Valley.

The majority of the items distributed in the Springfield area of Page County were bolts of cloth used to make clothing, bedding and blankets. They also provided cutlery, household goods and basic foodstuffs. Although the provision of material goods was a generous act, the need was so great that it only began to ameliorate the loss. The relief allotment for Peter Bixler provides a good example of the amount of formal assistance that was received in this area. Bixler was mentioned by name in the *Page Courier* after losing his entire house and worldly possessions. According to the 1870 census, he was a seventy-four-year-old white shoemaker who lived with his wife, Susan(seventy), and cared for their eleven-year-old grandson, Peter Glenn.[629] When relief came to the Bixler family, they were given the following:

> *1 comfort, 2 blankets, 9 yds ticking, 7½ yds sheeting cotton, 8 yds sheeps gray, 1 tea-kettle, 1 coffee mill, 1 bed mug, 6½ cotton flannel, 1 spool boss, 1 bunch thread, 1 dozen buttons, 3 yards brown cotton, 6 plates, 3 cups, 3 saucers, 1 dish, 1 bowl, 1 paper sugar, 1 do. coffee, 1 hat, ½ dozen buttons.*[630]

It is worthy to note that the distribution committee paid close attention to household needs and provided the Bixler family with exactly three cups and saucers, one for each member of the household. For those who received distributions of material goods, monetary disbursements ranged from fifty cents to ten dollars, with some, like Peter Bixler, receiving only physical goods.[631] It took about one to two months for goods and money to be received and distributed. When the Corn Exchange visited in October, Page County's relief committee had already distributed around $300 received from Baltimore.[632] The relief committee acknowledged the receipt of physical goods and a limited amount of money on November 27, 1870.[633] Therefore, the distribution took place sometime between November 27 and December 16, when the distribution for Springfield Township was recorded in the *Page Courier*.[634]

The Bixler family's relief distribution was one of the larger allotments. Although they did not receive any money, they were given a sizeable amount of physical goods from the Committee of the Corn Exchange. From this example and the other Page County distributions, it becomes apparent that the donations obtained by the Legislative Relief Committee were absolutely insufficient. Without the efforts of the Corn Exchange, along with funds from Baltimore and Philadelphia the sufferers in the county would have been in an extremely dire state. The Virginia Legislative Relief Committee acknowledged the deficit of funds in its October 26 appeal for relief. The total amount of donations received was much smaller than expected. Two of the potential contributing causes of the reduced amount of donations were inflated donation reports and the delay in active fundraising due to the statewide mourning following the death of General Robert E. Lee on October 12, 1870.

INFLATED DONATIONS AND THE DEATH OF GENERAL ROBERT E. LEE

The Virginia Legislative Committee's official "Appeal for Aid," published in various newspapers around October 26, 1870, acknowledges the distraction that mourning created for the entire state. Although the committee's membership and structure were finalized on October 10, its charitable work ground to a halt two days into the work when Lee's death was announced. The first few paragraphs of the "Appeal for Relief" reference the devastation and intense mourning that occurred in Virginia. The scale of grief for those on the committee was evidently sufficient to cease all relief work for the destitute to allow time for them to mourn. The committee explained that the members

> had scarcely assumed their duties when the hearts of the people, already sore and bleeding from their recent afflictions, were stricken with overwhelming anguish by the announcement of the death of General Lee. While the corpse of her best beloved son lay cold upon her bosom, the State could not bethink her for the time of the bereavements of her children, and all other tasks were laid aside, all other griefs forgotten, that we might commune and mourn together in our common sorrow, and do honor to our illustrious dead.[635]

From this statement, the intense mourning for General Lee appears to have diverted the official committee from its duty to the poor and destitute from approximately October 12 to October 26.

The scale of mourning was immense and reflected in every regional newspaper consulted. Several cities, including Richmond, Alexandria, Norfolk and Lynchburg, ceased business for the day when news of his death arrived.[636] Alexandria's city council passed several resolutions for how the city

Washington College colonnade draped in black mourning cloth after the death of Robert E. Lee. If you look closely, you can see that the recessed areas of the square columns have an added border of black cloth. *Image used with the permission of the Virginia Military Archives.*

would officially mourn, including that public buildings would be draped in mourning for thirty days, merchants and businesses were requested to close for the day of the funeral and the town bell was to be tolled "at intervals of three minutes on the day of the funeral."[637] In response to the news, papers across the state devoted several columns or even pages to remembrances of General Lee. There was also a visible change in story prominence as the remembrances and calls for a memorial fund to place a statue in Richmond eclipsed the appeals for aid and relief. Before the statewide committee could get back on track and publish their plan for relief, the *Daily Dispatch* reported that the "Lee Memorial Association" had already "been fully organized."[638]

When one looks through Governor Walker's papers, most of the large individual flood relief donations occur before October 15. A few donations that involve community collections are received after this point, such as the City of Norfolk collecting almost $650; however, the majority of the fundraising was completed within a few weeks after the flood. Grief and a shift in story prominence appear to have contributed to the derailment of official relief fundraising in Virginia.

In addition to grief, an erroneous report of extravagant donations from New York organizations also circulated in newspapers across Virginia during this time. The report appears to have originated in the *Baltimore Sun* on October 10, 1870. It is brief, but states, "The Stock Exchange has given $25,000 to the sufferers by the Virginia floods, the Gold Exchange $10,000, and the Merchants and Brokers' $15,000 more."[639] The idea that rich entities covered the cost of relief may have led some potential donors to abstain from individually participating in relief efforts, especially if potential donors had little expendable money.

Newspapers never revealed to the public that the New York Stock Exchange (NYSE) report was completely false. The minutes of the NYSE Governing Committee reveal that the committee received a request to aid to the Virginia and Harpers Ferry sufferers. The request was considered on October 7 and adopted for further discussion with 129 ayes and 65 nays. The committee revisited the matter on October 12 and concluded that a donation would violate a resolution passed earlier in the year that concluded "it was inexpedient to entertain any applications for donations from any source, other than that of relief for members of the New York Stock Exchanges and Whereas the condition of the finances of this institution and its contemplated expenditures do not warrant the Committee in departing from the rule then adopted."[640] It was therefore resolved that the NYSE would respectfully decline the request for aid as an organization.

In the same article from the *Baltimore Sun*, the Gold Exchange and the Merchants' Exchanges were reported to have given $10,000 and $15,000, respectively, to the cause. This inflated claim is erroneous. A letter in Governor Walker's papers confirms that the Gold Exchange donated $2,000, not $10,000.[641] The *New York Times* also publicly noted that the $2,000 donation was unanimously supported in a Gold Exchange vote on October 6 and reconfirmed the information in another article several days later. Additionally, there are no records that indicate the Merchants' Exchange donated any amount to the cause. As such, it appears that only $2,000 of the reported $50,000 donation was actually received. Some newspapers, like the *Rockingham Register*, correctly reported the $2,000 donation.[642] On November 28, Governor Walker made another call for funds that mentioned the error. In admitting the error, he acknowledged that the contributions had "somehow been greatly overestimated."[643] It took an "inquiry at the Executive Department of the State Government" for the lack of funds to come to light.[644] With a committee that should have been auditing receipts, this is a gross oversight that harmed a lot of people. This overblown total could have undermined fundraising, prompting several localities not to engage in relief efforts. The donation from the Gold Exchange also included a request for the money to be split between Virginia and West Virginia. The request was worded so that Governor Walker could use his discretion and judgment as to where the money would be best spent. It is likely that Harpers Ferry received little, if any, of the funds from this donation, as it was already in the process of being forever severed from Virginia.[645]

RELIEF IN HARPERS FERRY

The Harper's Ferry Relief Committee was composed of several prominent local businessmen. The committee was called into action on October 8, 1870, with the explicit purpose of attending to the needs of those who escaped the flood. The committee was proactive in its solicitation of donations and immediately contacted larger metropolitan areas, such as Baltimore and New York. These efforts were judiciously rewarded. By October 15, the committee had received $1,679.55 in cash donations along with clothing and food items.[646] The amount received is more than half of what the Virginia Legislative Relief Fund raised by October 26. Two weeks later, Frederick City, Maryland, donated "$1,052 in cash and $500 worth of clothing" to Harpers Ferry.[647]

There was also a Ladies Committee that raised $200 by October 15. The committee worked with haste and reported on October 25 that all received money and goods had been distributed. Since the leaders acknowledged that not all of the needs had been met, they stated that more aid was needed and would be accepted by any of the ladies on the committee.[648] Although it appears that the Ladies' Committee was more active in publicly calling meetings and passing resolutions, it was not given autonomy. Their chairman was a Dr. J.V. Simmons

The larger relief committee did not disclose the distribution of its funds or goods in a timely fashion. As a result, some members of the community became concerned and called for immediate publication of the full receipts and distributions. A public meeting was called on December 15 to address questions about the distribution of aid. A local businessman, John W. Neer, was chosen to serve as president of the counter-committee.[649] The meeting called for the relief committee to prepare an account of its contributions and disbursals for publication in the newspaper. The public's disgust with the lack of action was apparent, and the counter-committee called for immediate resolution: "This is deemed such an important duty on their part as cannot be avoided without imminent disgrace."[650] When several weeks passed without acknowledgement of the inquiry, a rather odd incident occurred. Instead of following up in the two papers that ran the initial inquiry, minutes of the counter-committee were submitted for publication in the *Baltimore American* newspaper.

The article was pointedly titled "The Disaster at Harper's Ferry—What Has Become of the Relief Fund?" and placed a second request for relief disclosure, noting that it had been over a month since the previous request. The meeting claimed that several citizens who were affected by the flood "have received nothing from these contributions" and wished to know what happened to the fund. The proceedings then called out the relief committee members by name and accused them of misappropriating funds. In scathing language, the counter-committee demanded

> *that the general and current rumors that several gentlemen of Harper's Ferry have received large sums of money, subscribed and designed for the relief of all sufferers by the flood, be inquired into, for the reason that said sums of money are in like manner reported to have been converted to the personal use of the persons [for] whom it was transmitted, and has never reached the beneficiaries.*[651]

The counter-committee went one step further by threatening legal action against the Harper's Ferry Relief Committee. It retained A.M. Kitemiller, attorney-at-law, to "represent the people, in all matters connected with this subject."[652] Kitemiller, likely a misspelling of Archibald Kitzmiller, was also listed as the secretary for this meeting and, as such, was authorized to publish the proceedings. Once published, further intrigue ensued by way of the *Shepherdstown Register*.

The *Shepherdstown Register* expressed disapproval at the actions of the counter-committee and ran a retraction of the "serious and damaging charge."[653] The article in the *Baltimore American* must have served its intended purpose to cause outrage and elicit a response from the Harper's Ferry Relief Committee. However, the response may have been more than John W. Neer had bargained for. Following the report, Neer and others in the counter-committee signed a paper "retracting the language attributed to them in the resolution, which, they say, were prepared and published without their knowledge and consent."[654]

While it is possible that the later report was published without their consent, the form of publication included resolutions, which appear to have been voted on within a committee setting. The public questioning of the actions of the business elite and leaders of Harpers Ferry may have caused severe backlash and repercussions for the counter-committee. While the motivations for retracting the statement may never fully be known, the public dissent called into question the overall responsibility of the relief committee and may have ultimately held them more accountable.

Several months later, on April 15, 1871, the *Virginia Free Press* finally published the relief committee's report of all of receipts and distributions. In regards to monetary distributions, John Wernwag, the spry machinist who floated down the river on the roof of his shop, received $151.35. The Reverend W.B. Dutton, who lost his home, suffered a traumatic head injury and was rescued by basket, was given $150. James Shipe, who lost his home and wife, Annie, while enduring a harrowing ordeal of swimming house to house received $50. Mrs. Nunnamaker, who lived on Shenandoah Street, was granted $150, while Mrs. Beecroft, who also lived in that vicinity, received only $11. Their rescuer, James T. Reed, who put saving lives above his business interests, was granted nothing. Finally, the counter-committee president, John W. Neer, also received nothing. The total amount of distributions equated $4,518.61.[655] It's possible that those excluded received physical goods, but no distribution list was published for that type of relief. From the exclusions on the list and lack of transparency, it's understandable that some in the community were concerned about equity and fairness in regards to the distributions.

The public dissent about the distribution of funds in Harpers Ferry shares similarities with the elite-run relief efforts of both the Mill River and Chicago communities. Mill River's relief efforts began with an attempt to nominate representatives from each town but ended with the normal handful of wealthy elites.[656] Their relief efforts ended up being lorded over by a finance committee run by the reservoir company, which had final say about relief expenditures.[657] The Chicago Relief and Aid Society was led by a group of elite businessmen who subscribed to a relief ideology that posited the working class should not become dependent on charity or alms.[658] They believed the threat of dependency could lead to social disorder and upheaval, which was to be avoided at all costs. According to Sidney Gay, a former director of the fire relief society, if relief was not distributed properly, "the laboring people of Chicago, instead of being cheerfully at work at good wages, would have been at this very moment a starving, discontented, turbulent population."[659]

The Chicago Relief and Aid Society felt it had a duty to uphold social order and deemed it acceptable to withhold aid from those it they found unfit. The method of distribution was met with dissent in a published letter to a Chicago newspaper. The writer claimed that the society "failed to do what they agreed to do by taking care of suffering humanity." Further, "millions from all parts of the globe have sent their donations here to relieve those in distress, and not to be hoarded and lorded over by a set of men whose sympathies are foreign to the task at hand."[660] The writer of this article shared similar opinions with the Harpers Ferry counter-committee. While relegated to a much smaller scale, those in Harpers Ferry in need of assistance were at the mercy of the judgment of the wealthy elite. Without oversight and published accounts of the work, it is understandable why the public would have been concerned with the livelihoods of so many people at stake.[661]

RICHMOND, VIRGINIA

Richmond's response to the flood was significantly different from all other affected locations. In contrast to most other heavily impacted parts of the state, the city of Richmond did not have a dedicated relief committee that solicited donations for local sufferers or the statewide relief committee. The reasons why Richmond did not form a local relief committee are unclear. However, it is likely due to the circumstances surrounding its flood warning and preparation, prevalent social theories pertaining to aid and potentially the belief that the statewide committee had successfully raised enough funds. A combination of these factors in varying degrees likely influenced the way that relief was thought about and executed in Richmond at this time.

Although many people lost homes and property in the city and in Manchester on the Chesterfield County side of the James River, there is no recorded loss of life in this location.[662] The advance warning that saved the lives of the citizens also allowed many residents and business owners to move material goods out of the reach of the floodwaters, greatly reducing the overall loss to the city. However, even with the benefit of preparation, the *Richmond Whig* and the *Richmond Dispatch* estimated that material losses solely to local businesses in the city aggregated to approximately $42,275 and $54,100.[663] These figures are based on the printed lists in the newspapers of estimated losses to individual merchants.

Although merchants along the Shockoe Bottom and lower parts of the city suffered monetary and material good loss, there was also quite a lot of domestic and mercantile damage in the Rocketts Landing and Manchester areas. The *Richmond Dispatch* noted, "Rocketts suffered perhaps more than any other part of the city."[664] Even though this area was both an active

The St. Charles Hotel was once a landmark in Richmond. The building was torn down in the late 1890s in order to construct Main Street Station. *Engraving from* Frank Leslie's Illustrated Newspaper, *October 22, 1870. Scanned from original.*

wharf and domestic location, the newspaper coverage often glosses over the specifics pertaining to the domestic loss. A methodical account of damaged dwellings or domestic sufferers was not reported in either the *Richmond Whig* or the *Richmond Dispatch*, which significantly contrasts with their coverage of merchant losses. Both papers devoted several column inches to listing specific names and damage amounts for businesses in the area.[665]

An article devoted to the domestic loss in the *Richmond Whig* reveals that an estimated twenty houses in the Rocketts vicinity and several houses in Manchester were completely carried away by the floodwaters while many more were significantly damaged. The *Whig* reported on the tenacity of the people who lived along the river and their efforts to rebuild. After the flood, the sufferers who camped on the Richmond hills while waiting for the water to recede "waded through mud knee-deep to find their dwellings, if standing, wrecked in many instances beyond permanent repair, their furniture scattered and broken and their stock of food swept away."[666] The area was in such ruin that the *Whig* commented, "Words are not adequate to task of picturing the desolation and ruin which has occurred among the poor people living in the submerged districts."[667] The vivid and sympathetic depiction is contrasted by the *Richmond Dispatch*, which did not report a number of lost dwellings but commented that "no houses of value in and around the town have been swept away."[668] The language of this phrase is dismissive to the residents of Rocketts, who worked hard to accumulate basic comforts and whose homes held personal value. The *Whig* contrasts this sentiment by explaining to their readers that the people of Rocketts,

> *Through years of toil and privation manage annually in some way or another to collect around them plain furniture, little comforts and modest luxuries—simple in themselves, but all the world to them, because they are their all of wealth.*[669]

The Rocketts Landing area was mainly inhabited by African Americans and immigrants, many of whom survived on limited means. The discussion of their losses is often accompanied by lightly veiled or even overt racism. Although Rocketts was acknowledged as the place that received the most destruction in Richmond, none of the sufferers were mentioned by name except Landrum Henderson, who actually lived on the Manchester side.[670] Henderson's plight is referenced in both the *Richmond Whig* and the *New York Herald*. In the *Herald*, he is referred to as a "well-to-do negro" who "had just erected a handsome residence and furnished it in a style magnificent for one of his race."[671] The article then describes the destruction of his house and ended the story with a dubious phonetic-style quote attributed to Henderson: "Well, dar, dat's done gone; but de Lor's will be done; ol' Mas'r knows what's the bestest." The quote is reprinted here because it is the only attributed reaction from an identifiable African American source pertaining to the flood. However, it is hard to believe that Henderson spoke these words, especially as a former corporal in the Union army. It is plausible that the *Herald* created this quote to coincide with its other racist commentary, including an account of supposed superstitious practices that African Americans engaged in during the flood. Although there is no way to verify intent, it is clear that most newspapers were not in the business of soliciting aid or sympathy for the victims in this location. The *Richmond Whig* is the exception. After describing their plight, they remind their readers, "unless the charitable give them immediate assistance there must be great suffering among them."[672] The *Whig* also points out that the business community often excludes their importance as customers, noting that "their aggregate subsistence amounts to a round sum when listed."[673]

Despite the obvious need, there were few calls for charity and relief in Richmond following the flood. In the immediate wake, the Academy of Music proposed to donate the "receipts of the house" for the benefit of flood victims on Friday, October 7.[674] However, nothing is mentioned regarding the outcome. It is unknown if the donation actually took place or how successful it might have been. In a similar vein, on October 28, the *Richmond Dispatch* promoted a lecture from which the receipts would be given to the statewide relief committee. There were also periodic references regarding donations to the Legislative Relief Committee by entities outside of the city, but nothing specifically relating to a local committee for the Richmond area. Although the *Whig* made a point to comment about the urgency and need for aid, no appeals pertaining to a local aid committee were printed in either the *Richmond Whig* or the *Richmond Dispatch*.

After the flood, those living in the Rocketts area worked to salvage furniture and goods from the river. Here someone is testing a valuable piano for water damage while three men attempt to retrieve something heavy from the water. Notice the houses and debris in the water. *Engraving from* Frank Leslie's Illustrated Newspaper, *October 22, 1870. Scanned from original.*

It appears that Richmond was disinclined to form a committee or formally organize local relief. The *Whig* reported on the committee proceedings of the Norfolk Relief Committee and the Legislative Relief Committee, which indicates that the paper was not ignoring any potential relief efforts. However, there were no printed appeals requesting the formation of a local committee or solicitations for donations in the city. At first, it seems possible that the citizens of Richmond may have felt that the Legislative Relief Committee would do a better job of providing and distributing relief because two of their representatives were appointed to serve on the joint committee. However, the Legislative Relief Committee was not actually formed until ten days after the flood, when all other locations consulted had already begun making preparations for alleviating the needs of the local sufferers.

It is also possible that Victorian social ideas pertaining to morality and poverty may have shaped and influenced the relief efforts in the city of Richmond. At this point in time, relief thought had evolved to include the idea of the "undeserving poor."[675] This concept generally excludes certain segments of the population from aid due to the belief that they are unworthy due to various moral, cultural or biological attributes.[676] However, what is considered "undeserving" has varied throughout history. At its most general definition, it excludes those who are believed to be able-bodied individuals. However, other segments of the population are often excluded depending on prevailing social, political or economic influences.

Additionally, there was a moral component that guided beliefs pertaining to the "underserving poor." During the late eighteenth and early nineteenth century, the idea of pauperism resulting from deficiencies of morality began to rise and influence charitable thought. According to historian Michael Katz, "The redefinition of poverty as a moral condition accompanied the transition to capitalism and democracy in early nineteenth century America."[677] In Richmond, it appears that the sufferers of the flood were denied at least some portion of relief or active fundraising due to the belief that those who lost their homes had the perceived moral affliction of being "thriftless."[678]

Certain phrases and terms pertaining to the domestic sufferers' plight in the Rocketts area appear to support this hypothesis. On October 4, in its only mention of aid for the Rocketts area, the *Richmond Whig* noted, "It will not do to say that some of them are thriftless, and therefore, not deserving and on that account, withhold aid from all."[679] Here, the *Whig* appealed to its readership to help the poor. However, it made the point to acknowledge that some community members may have believed that the sufferers were undeserving and that this was a legitimate concern as a basis for withholding aid. To make a statement of this nature indicates that a significant portion of the *Whig*'s readership must have regarded at least some residents of Rocketts as the "undeserving poor."

The official Richmond city ordinances also reveal a general attitude toward and methods of sanctioned aid for the poor. The Ordinances of the City of Richmond were rewritten in 1869 and contain a section specifically devoted to the "The Poor" of the city. The pages outline the specific requirements guiding the administration and admission to the almshouse. Within this, there are stipulations that the applicants must be "proper subjects" to receive aid.[680] The ordinance does not specify the requirements of a "proper subject" beyond stipulating that he or she must be a resident of Richmond for at least one full year. In keeping with contemporary aid practices, Richmond was concerned about caring only for established residents of the city. To avoid an influx of vagrants and the extra financial burden for caring for the poor who came from other locations, Richmond had strict rules and fines to reduce this aspect of relief expenditure. Although the ordinance does not paint a clear picture of how Richmond cared for its own citizens, examining the disaster that occurred at the capitol in April 1870 may offer a better understanding of the culture of relief in Richmond.

On April 27, 1870, the second floor of the Virginia Capitol collapsed, killing 60 people and injuring approximately 120.[681] The Richmond Chamber of Commerce formed a committee two days later on April 29, 1870. According to its minute book, the committee met almost every day until June 29, 1870. It raised a total of $80,603.58 and dispersed the funds to those who were permanently injured, widowed or dependents of the deceased.[682] This effort shows how effective and swift fundraising in Richmond could be for a cause or segment of the population deemed worthy. While this was a condensed local disaster, the overall number of casualties and those rendered financially destitute is somewhat equitable to those sustained throughout the entire geographic impact of the 1870 flood.[683] It is possible that the disbursement of flood victims across the state conflicted with Richmond's priority of mainly caring for its established residents. The priority of caring for Richmond's own sufferers would explain the lack of aid solicitation and donations to the Legislative Relief Committee. However, it does not explain the absence of a local committee.

It is also plausible that the recent large-scale fundraising in the city for the capitol disaster victims left the citizens in a position where they were overtaxed and unable to contribute to the sufferers in Rocketts. The lack of funds may have played a pivotal role in the dearth of donated relief. However, it appears many pocketbooks found suitable leverage to fundraise for another cause. The Robert E. Lee statue that would eventually be placed on Monument Avenue received support from Richmonders in late October 1870 at least in terms of calls for fundraising and organizing committees.[684] If the citizens of Richmond were able to donate money for a statue, it appears that the lack of local relief may have been due to personal opinions about the "undeserving poor" or that the quick clean-up removed the flood from the thoughts of the potential donors.

Finally, it is possible that Richmond handled the situation differently because the flood did not visibly affect the great majority of the city. An article published on October 7 reveals this sentiment: "We took a stroll by the river yesterday and were astonished to find that the streets along the dock and leading to the wharves show so little trace of the late flood."[685] To expedite clean-up, Richmond utilized a chain gang to quickly clean up the streets and remove debris. Once the visible damage had been removed from the areas of the city the elite would traverse, it seems that the flood was forgotten by many citizens as they moved on with their lives.

Days after the flood, the *Richmond Whig* published an article promoting self-sufficiency and fortitude in the face of destruction. It recommended avoiding surrendering to despair as a remedy to the devastation. Those who were injured must "summon all their fortitude, rally all their energies, and go to work again."[686] By the wording, the column was written by a Richmonder. The sentiment may have been an early incarnation of the "Virginia Way," which lauds self-sufficiency and a rejection of charity. Although the writer offered a noble sentiment, it did nothing to alleviate the needs of the sufferers who faced starvation, exposure to the elements, potential bankruptcy, jailtime for vagrancy, and even death. There are no known records of how relief came to this city, but it is apparent that it did not take place under the aegis of a local flood relief committee.

THE OTHER LOCATIONS EXAMINED throughout the state fostered a spirit of charity. Page County, Harpers Ferry and Alexandria's Committee of the Corn Exchange all worked hard to solicit donations and provide as much relief as possible. Lynchburg also espoused these ideals in the media but fell short when donations were desperately needed. Unfortunately, a series of failures within the organizational structure caused the total amount of donations to be significantly less than what was needed to help all of the people who were rendered destitute. Even the more successful committees were unable to take care for all victims or provide substantial relief for rebuilding lives. The Committee of the Corn Exchange was likely the most beneficial to those living in the Shenandoah Valley. The statewide committee ground to a halt following the death of General Lee, which caused a discernable distraction from the charitable work and was publicly acknowledged as a contributing failure to the effort. When coupled with artificially inflated donation amounts, beliefs about the "undeserving poor" and an already financially strained populace, the entire effort fell short. It is impossible to point to a single cause as the point of overwhelming failure, but it becomes clear that the needs of thousands of people were not met. Henry Wiltse, despite overwhelming loss, was lucky to have friends and neighbors he could rely on to help him in the immediate aftermath of the storm and may have fared better than those in other regions of the state. When the floodwaters receded, a new landscape with overwhelming obstacles became the reality for hundreds of people who sought aid and received insufficient funds.

5

MEMORY AND MEMORIALIZATION

M r. Quick passed a square-cut granite post lying on the ground near the north end of Mayo's bridge "plenty of times" during his nineteen years of working as a Southern Railway yard clerk. He regarded it as part of the terrain—something that had always been there. In 1936, his curiosity was piqued when a crew working on a new coal trestle was told that there might be "a written record of a last-century high-water mark on the underside." A few members of the crew decided to flip the nearly thousand-pound granite post over using crowbars "out of idle curiosity" and were surprised to find "a bronze tablet bolted on near the top" with an inscription marking the high-water line of the 1870 flood.[687]

Prior to 1877, the citizens of Richmond deemed it important enough to memorialize the high-water mark of the 1870 flood with a pillar out of granite and bronze. The shock and devastation that was left in its wake caused changes to be made that would ameliorate some of the effects of future flooding. Like Staunton widening the channel for Lewis Creek after mild flooding in 1860, knowing the danger that was possible caused some proactive changes to be made. For instance, the Dutch-Gap canal was enlarged and "many of the obstructions in the river were removed."[688] Additionally, heavily damaged places like the Shenandoah Iron Works were rebuilt further from the water. Although the 1877 flood was similar in range, height and affected areas, it wasn't as deadly. It caused comparable damage to railroads, bridges, canals, mills and some farms, but not to the extent of the 1870 floodwaters.

The granite pillar stood in front of the St. Charles Hotel on Main Street possibly until the hotel was demolished to make way for Main Street Station in 1901 or when Fourteenth Street was widened around 1911.[689] Its demise may be associated with similar and higher flooding in 1877 and 1889, making the marker less relevant as a unique event and may be a symbolic representation of the 1870 flood sinking into the recesses of history. Prior to the floodwall completion in 1994, there were many flooding events that shaped Richmond's history, including two hundred-year floods, both of which received markers. A monument commemorating the 1771 flood was erected on Turkey Island by the Randolph family in 1772. The marker is a brick obelisk inscribed, "The foundation of the pillar was laid in the calamitous year, 1771, when all the great Rivers of this country were swept by inundations never before experienced which changed the face of Nature and left traces of their violence which will last for Ages."[690]

The Turkey Island marker is likely the oldest extant flood commemoration in Virginia. It is particularly important because its existence may signify a change in the way that people thought about floods and the need for historic remembrance. It also may have influenced Richmonders to commemorate the 1870 flood event with a marker because of repeated comparisons to the 1771 flood and knowledge of the earlier marker. It is not uncommon for relevance and meaning to change over the course of time. Repeated flooding often makes it difficult to keep track of the various flood events. Even with reduced prominence, knowledge of the 1870 flood often rears its head during times of subsequent flooding, marking its importance to local memory in short and intermittent spurts.

In parts of the Shenandoah Valley, the 1870 flood is often the preeminent event to which subsequent floods are compared. Its devastation is a part of local legend, most often recalled in passing during the wake of a later flood event. Although it occurred 150 years ago, the ripples were felt long after the event faded into memory. Through the loss of lives, buildings, structures, personal property and even certain landscapes, communities were permanently altered. Although it is nearly impossible to study the effect on each of the individuals within the affected communities, there are noticeable patterns of physical changes to structures and building practices that resulted in long-term changes to communities in terms of transportation, accessibility and the location of new buildings.

Some of the structural losses resulted in changes to building practices, such as higher bridges and dwellings built farther away from waterways, which benefitted the affected areas during subsequent floods. Alternatively, some structural losses, such as the Chain Bridge near Georgetown and White House Bridge in Page County, were not immediately repaired, rerouting transportation for several years. At White House Bridge, traffic was accommodated by a pay ferry until the bridge was rebuilt during the 1910s, which may have influenced the economic landscape in the immediate area for decades.[691]

Hundreds of families suffered economic hardships and were granted only a pittance of relief. It is almost impossible to measure the effects of the economic losses for individuals, but most assuredly, some families went bankrupt and others relocated. On an individual or community level, the suffering endured by the families who lost loved ones and personal property or experienced environmental damage to the immediate surrounding landscape most often manifested as local histories and stories. However, several places that were heavily affected by the flood also erected monuments or museum exhibits that either memorialize the dead or discuss the damage to the immediate area. The memorials and historic discussions are nuanced and filled with meaning and memory.

The communities that received the brunt of the damage often memorialized the 1870 flood through markers that commemorate lost community or family members, like the Kite Memorial in Page County, or recorded the height of the water, as in Richmond. The 1870 flood is also marked in areas that received repeated historic flooding, such as Scottsville or Harpers Ferry. These markers serve as a way to remember the disastrous events that repeatedly shaped community life along the waterways.

In Page County, sixty-eight years after the flood, a memorial was dedicated to the Noah Kite family on September 1, 1938.[692] According to contemporary reports, over three hundred people attended the dedication, which included a program of speakers and the formal unveiling of the memorial located near the original house site. The event was advertised in local newspapers several months in advance.[693] The planning and care that went into making the memorial happen is especially poignant when one considers that fundraising for the marker took place during the midst of the Great Depression. Those who spearheaded the commemorative monument were relatives of the Noah Kite family who began planning for the memorial after a large family reunion that took place during the summer of 1937.[694] The reasons for the memorial at this particular point in time are unclear. However, it is possible that a nationwide drop in unemployment during 1937 may have contributed to the ability to fundraise or travel to a larger family reunion at this point in time.[695] Plausibly, a larger reunion, more readily

Kite Family Memorial, Alma, Virginia, 2015. The original stone marker was dedicated in 1938. The current one was replaced about 1996 after Hurricane Fran. *Photo by author.*

available funds (compared to previous years) and the involvement of Noah and Isabella Kite's grandchildren (who would have been in their fifties and sixties) likely all played a role in the timing.

The nearly six-foot-tall granite memorial was engraved with the names of the Kite family members who passed away during the flood and is surrounded with a wrought-iron fence. The periphery of the memorial is encircled with a masonry stonework fence and stairs that lead from the road. In recent years, the original stone has been replaced with a new marker of machine-cut granite. The recent replacement shows continued care and the lingering importance of this memorial to its caretakers.

Although the marker is privately maintained by family members, it also has meaning for the larger community. The stone and stories of the events surrounding the Kite family's demise are part of the local lore and public knowledge about flooding events in Page County. Every time there is a major flood in the area, the tale of Noah Kite and his family's tragic death is revisited in local newspapers. Sometimes the tale will lie dormant for years before regaining public relevance for a printed retelling. In 1985, the events were discussed in detail in the wake of a large flood that was considered to be one of the worst to hit the Page Valley. This article went into detail about the differences between the 1870 and 1877 floods and how they affected the community. It also discussed the different flood depths and damage, which helped place the most recent flood event into the larger context of historic flooding in the area.

When Hurricane Fran struck in September 1996, the 1870 flood and the events near Honeyville were once again a part of the local newspaper coverage and a reminder that Page County had seen worse. The 1996 articles referred to the 1870 flood as "the worst flood to hit Page County." At that point in time, it was generally accepted that the flooding as a result of Hurricane Fran was the second-worst flood in the history of the county, surpassing 1985, which had held that distinction for eleven years.

The comparison to other historic flooding events or local natural disasters may in part be a way of coping with a present disaster. A sense of comfort may lie in knowing that others have gone through similar trials. Additionally, knowledge and discussion of a historic disaster can be a part of the local "sense of place" and contribute to understanding how the environment historically shaped the social, economic and physical landscape. The stories may serve as a way to exhibit community longevity and tie in a sense of community that resonates with longtime residents. These flooding events are a part of the local history and often remain in the shadows, waiting to be used as a comparison or point of reference for a future flood.

In the town of Scottsville in Albemarle and Fluvanna County, the history of the town's flooding takes on a prominent part of the local open-air museum. A brick and stone marker displays the various heights of the "Floods of Record" for the town beginning in 1771 and ending in 1987. The marker recorded the height of the 1870 flood as 30.7 feet. Although the marker records thirteen major floods, the 1870 flood is the fourth highest.[696] The 1870 flood also appears to be regarded as a point of reference for modern flooding. The Scottsville Museum's website claims that the town "has experienced twenty-one floods of 20 feet or more above mean low water level" since the 1870 flood.[697]

Scottsville flood marker, Scottsville, Virginia, 2015. This marker is prominently displayed in Canal Basin Square. *Photo by author.*

The recorded quantity of flooding has adversely affected the town throughout its history, making it difficult to isolate the effect of a singular flood event. However, the open-air canal exhibit references the combined effect of 1870 and 1877 on the canal system. The exhibit explains, "Despite the committed support of powerful commercial and political interests, plans for the extension of the canal were abandoned. Extensive flood damage in the 1870s forced closings of the canal and underscored the high cost of repairing and maintaining the canal."[698] The marker also mentions a levee that was completed in 1989 and reduced the need for future flood recording in the town. According to the Scottsville Museum, the town has not been flooded since the completion of the levee thirty-one years ago.[699]

Although general knowledge of the 1870 flood has all but faded into history, the study of its aftermath, economic impact and distribution of aid reveals a great deal about regional life in Virginia and West Virginia during Reconstruction. As a case study, it shows how the examination of media coverage and charitable aid in response to a natural disaster can be used to better understand different facets of regional political, economic and social history. Even though the flood took place 150 years ago, it was an important event that shaped the lives of those who encountered waters that caused "a scene of ruin and desolation…scarcely paralleled."[700]

Appendix A

KNOWN CASUALTIES OF THE 1870 FLOOD

Names	Age (if known)	Gender	Ethnicity	Location
Virginia				
Agee Benjamin	17	male	White	Columbia, Fluvanna Co.
Aleshire, Robert	28	male	White	Honeyville, Page Co.
Allen, Lizzie		female	White	Mt. Jackson, Shenandoah Co.
Blakemore, Elzora	10	female	White	Front Royal, Warren Co.
Blakemore, Flora	6	female	White	Front Royal, Warren Co.
Blakemore, Mary	47	female	White	Front Royal, Warren Co.
Blakemore, Mary Helen	14	female	White	Front Royal, Warren Co.
Blakemore, Thomas A.	46	male	White	Front Royal, Warren Co.

Names	Age (if known)	Gender	Ethnicity	Location
Breeding, Nicholas		male		Page Co.
Buckner, Eliza	24	female	African American	Lynchburg, Campbell Co.
Buckner, John	8	male	African American	Lynchburg, Campbell Co.
Buckner, Mary	1	female	African American	Lynchburg, Campbell Co.
Buckner, Samuel	6	male	African American	Lynchburg, Campbell Co.
Burke, John	68	male	White	Shaw's Fork, Highland Co.
Cary, John	61	male	African American	Columbia, Fluvanna Co.
Cary, Peggy	45	female	African American	Columbia, Fluvanna Co.
Chamberlain, Charles	22	male	White	Strasburg, Frederick Co.
Davis, William H.	48	male	White	Columbia, Fluvanna Co.
Fuqua, Joseph	38	male	White	Columbia, Fluvanna Co.
Green, Ben		male	African American	Bridgewater, Rockingham Co.
Ham, Betsy	79	female	White	Weyer's Cave, Augusta Co.
Hammer, John A.		male	White	Elk Run, Rockingham
Hoskins, Mary A.	25	female	White	Front Royal, Warren Co.
Hoskins, Mary Ann	1yr, 6mo	female	White	Front Royal, Warren Co.

NAMES	AGE (IF KNOWN)	GENDER	ETHNICITY	LOCATION
young lady with Hoskins	youth	female	White	Front Royal, Warren Co.
Jennings child	youth		White	Rio Mills, Albemarle Co.
Jennings child	youth		White	Roi Mills, Albemarle Co
Johnson, Booker	youth	male	African American	Lynchburg, Campbell Co.
Jones, Judy	21	female	White	Norwood, Nelson Co.
Jones, William A.	26	male	White	Norwood, Nelson Co.
Kite, Ashby Jacob	8	male	White	Honeyville, Page Co.
Kite, Edward L.	6	male	White	Honeyville, Page Co.
Kite, Eudora	17	female	White	Honeyville, Page Co
Kite, Isabella	49	female	White	Honeyville, Page Co.
Kite, Noah	56	male	White	Honeyville, Page Co.
McCauley child			White	Rockingham Co.
Nauman, Elenora Kite	25	female	White	Honeyville, Page Co.
Ransom, Elvira J.	29	female	White	Lynchburg, Campbell Co.
Ransom, Lizzie	13	female	White	Lynchburg, Campbell Co.
Ridgeway, Jacqueline	22	female	White	Front Royal, Warren Co.
Roberts, Mrs.		female		Scottsville, Fluvanna Co.

Names	Age (if known)	Gender	Ethnicity	Location
Robinson, unknown		male	African American	Berry's Ferry, Clarke Co.
Simpson, Roberta	8yr, 3mo	female	White	Cedarville, Warren Co.
Smallwood, Sally	8	female	White	Cedarville, Warren Co.
Stoneburner, James	25	male	White	Honeyville, Page Co.
Ward, Martha	12	female	African American	Lynchburg, Campbell Co.
West, Augustus	59	male	White	Honeyville, Page Co.
Whitlow, Robinetta	10	female	White	Lynchburg, Campbell Co.
Whitlow, Sarah	8	female	White	Lynchburg, Campbell Co.
Whitlow, Willie	13	male	White	Lynchburg, Campbell Co.
Wiltse, Asley	8	male	White	Rio Mills, Albemarle Co.
Wiltse, Dolly	31	female	White	Rio Mills, Albemarle Co.
Wiltse, Henry	2	male	White	Rio Mills, Albemarle Co.
Woodson, Mrs.		female		Norwood, Nelson Co.
Woodson Child				Norwood, Nelson Co.
unidentified person on Woodson boat				Norwood, Nelson Co.
unidentified		male		Welfley's Mill, Page Co.

Names	Age (if known)	Gender	Ethnicity	Location
unidentified, Albert		male	African American	Snicker's Ferry, Clarke Co., Virginia
unidentified ferryman		male	White	Berry's Ferry, Clarke Co.
unidentified		male	African American	Castleman's Ferry, Clarke Co., Virginia
2 unidentified		male		Crossing Chain Bridge, Little Falls, Arlington Co., Virginia
2 unidentified		male	African American	near the Aqueduct Bridge, Georgetown, Maryland
unidentified		female	African American	Harrisonburg, Rockingham Co.
unidentified	child		African American	Harrisonburg, Rockingham Co.
West Virginia				
Bateman, Adam	43	male	African American	Bolivar, Jefferson Co.
Bateman, Benjamin	41	male	African American	Bolivar, Jefferson Co.
Bateman, Benjamin	1	male	African American	Bolivar, Jefferson Co.
Bateman, Elizabeth C.	30	female	African American	Bolivar, Jefferson Co.
Bateman, Emily	9	female	African American	Bolivar, Jefferson Co.
Bateman, Franny	4yr, 6mo	female	African American	Bolivar, Jefferson Co.

Names	Age (if known)	Gender	Ethnicity	Location
Bateman, James	45	male	African American	Bolivar, Jefferson Co.
Bateman, James	15	male	African American	Bolivar, Jefferson Co.
Bateman, James C.	6	male	African American	Bolivar, Jefferson Co.
Bateman, Julia	12	female	African American	Bolivar, Jefferson Co.
Bateman, Malcolm B.	8	male	African American	Bolivar, Jefferson Co.
*Bateman, Nancy	40	female	African American	Bolivar, Jefferson Co.
Bateman, Sarah	12	female	African American	Bolivar, Jefferson Co.
Bateman, Walter	10	male	African American	Bolivar, Jefferson Co.
Brady, John	20	male	African American	Harpers Ferry, Jefferson Co.
Brady "Girl"	child	female	African American	Harper's Ferry, Jefferson Co.
Carroll, Margaret	74	female	White	Harpers Ferry, Jefferson Co.
Harris, Adeline	4	female	African American	Bolivar, Jefferson Co.
Harris, Janetta	45	female	African American	Bolivar, Jefferson Co.
Harris, Jeremiah "Jere"	70	male	African American	Bolivar, Jefferson Co.
Harris, Rebecca	20	female	African American	Bolivar, Jefferson Co.
Harvey, Jacob	75	male	African American	Harpers Ferry, Jefferson Co.

Names	Age (if known)	Gender	Ethnicity	Location
Hoff, Samuel	28	male	White	Harpers Ferry, Jefferson Co.
Lewis, John D.	50	male	White	Rockford, Jefferson, Co.
Mills, Archibald	1	female	White	Harpers Ferry, Jefferson Co.
Mills, Catherine	38	female	While	Harpers Ferry, Jefferson Co.
Myers, Cora M.	1yr, 2mo	female	African American	Bolivar, Jefferson Co.
Myers, John Hinton	30	male	African American	Bolivar, Jefferson Co.
Myers, Hugh	4	male	African American	Bolivar, Jefferson Co.
Myers, Mary	28	female	African American	Bolivar, Jefferson Co.
Overton, Sarah	58	female	White	Harpers Ferry, Jefferson Co.
Philips, Emma	5	female	African American	Harpers Ferry, Jefferson Co.
Phillips, George	3	male	African American	Harpers Ferry, Jefferson Co.
Rust, Amelia	25	female	African American	Harpers Ferry, Jefferson Co.
Rust, William H.	1	male	African American	Harpers Ferry, Jefferson Co.
Shipe, Annie	27	female	White	Harpers Ferry, Jefferson Co.

Source: Census Records, Vital Records, Newspaper Accounts

*Nancy Bateman is included in the newspaper accounts but not on the official death records.

Appendix B

PETER BIXLER'S RELIEF ALLOTMENT

The Bixler family received one of sixteen distributions for the Springfield Township in Page County that was reported in the *Page Courier* on December 16, 1870.[701] Peter Bixler and his family were fortunate to have received a sizable relief allocation in terms of physical goods, and theirs is a good example of a larger relief portion. This photo is a modern compilation of the listed items based on the author's interpretation of the description. Although the items depicted are not 100 percent accurate, they help to illustrate an example of the limited resources that were parceled out to victims of the flood.

Peter Bixler's relief included:

1 COMFORT. Interpreted to mean a comforter. In the photo, it is located in the center, with a hat resting on it.

2 BLANKETS. The blankets are stacked to the left in the photo. Only the top crocheted blanket is visible.

9 YDS TICKING. Ticking was a blue-and-white cloth used for bedding. 9 yards were unavailable at the time the photo was taken, so its depiction is somewhat reduced. It is located second from the top of the cloth goods on the right.

7½ YDS SHEETING COTTON. Located on the top of the right stack of cloth goods.

8 YDS SHEEPS GRAY. Sheeps gray was a heavy cloth of undyed gray wool. The depicted item is located on the bottom of the right stack of cloth goods.

Modern representation of the Bixler family's relief allotment. Many of the goods were provided by the Alexandria Committee of Corn Exchange. *Photo by author.*

1 TEA-KETTLE. The style of and size of the kettle are not mentioned. Here, the item is represented with an iron kettle, which is located in the middle of the photo.

1 COFFEE MILL. The style of coffee mill is not listed. It is represented by an antique mill that may be a later model.

1 BED MUG. *Bed mug* is another term for a chamber pot. This item is depicted with an ironstone mug. However, the original would likely not have had a spouted lip.

6½ COTTON FLANNEL. "6½" was interpreted to mean 6½ yards. This cloth is located directly above the sheeps gray on the right.

1 SPOOL BOSS. Interpreted to mean a sewing spool, this item is depicted as a wooden spool in the foreground.

1 BUNCH THREAD. The allotment did not specify a color. Also, there was no specification for how much thread was in a "bunch." Although incorrect, the thread is depicted with white embroidery floss to illustrate a somewhat substantial amount of thread.

1 DOZEN BUTTONS. It is unknown what size, type or style of buttons were received. However, they were likely shell, metal or glass. Twelve $^3/_8$-inch four-holed shell buttons were used for the image.

3 YARDS BROWN COTTON. The brown cotton is located directly below the ticking on the right.

6 PLATES. It is unknown what type of plates were received and whether or not they matched. For the purpose of this photo, six matching ten-inch

Blue Willow–patterned plates were used. The Blue Willow pattern would have been available at this time.

3 CUPS. Three matching Blue Willow–patterned cups were included in the photo. However, the style of cup is likely not accurate for 1870.

3 SAUCERS. The photo includes three matching five-and-one-half-inch Blue Willow saucers.

1 DISH. It is unclear what type or size of dish was received. Unfortunately, the author only had a divided vegetable dish on hand. The original item was likely not divided. This represented dish is located toward the middle of the photo in the foreground.

1 BOWL. The size and style of the original bowl is unknown. For the purpose of this image, a nine-and-one-half-inch round Blue Willow bowl was included.

1 PAPER SUGAR. The term *paper sugar* generally refers to a cone-shaped compressed brick of sugar that was often covered in blue paper. The size of the paper sugar is unknown. There was a dearth of scholarship pertaining to the style of paper sugars available in 1870. As a result, an earlier stylistic model that was popular during the late eighteen century was used. It is located toward the middle of the photo between the coffee and iron kettle.

1 DO. COFFEE: One "do." likely refers to the number of ounces. Whole coffee beans were used in the depiction.

1 HAT. It is unclear what style of hat was received and whether or not it was for a man, woman or child. A straw hat made for a man is included in the image. However, it is likely not completely period appropriate.

½ DOZEN BUTTONS. Here again, it is unknown what size, type or style of buttons were received. Six half-inch four-holed shell buttons were chosen, which are located in the foreground of the photo near the spool boss and thread.

Appendix C
TRANSCRIPTIONS

TRANSCRIBED ARTICLE NO. 1

John D. Imboden, "The Late Flood," New York Herald,
October 4, 1870

The Late Flood
Project of Aid for the Sufferers.
The following letter from General Imboden is published and warmly
endorsed by the *New York Herald*:

New York, October 4, 1870
To the Editor of the Herald:
Sir—In your editorial comments this morning on the terrible calamity that
has just befallen so many of the long suffering, uncomplaining, struggling
people of my State—Virginia—you make a suggestion to this great and
wealthy city that I hope will be acted upon, and that some aid will be
rendered to the thousands of poor people, white and black, in the regions
swept by the late and unprecedented freshets. I am personally familiar with
the whole region drained by the James river and its tributaries and the
Shenandoah, and, from the accounts I have seen in the papers, as well as
private information from home, I am satisfied that the suffering entailed
upon the people, especially the poor, will be greater for a time than any

they endured in the (to them) most disastrous period of the war. The very means of daily subsistence have been swept away from thousands of people in a few hours. Crops, mills, and animals are all destroyed along the water courses in many of our fairest and best counties. Starvation stares thousands in the face unless prompt assistance and supplies are furnished. Our own people again, as in the past, will heal each other as fast and as liberally as possible, and probably no appeal will be heard coming from the sufferers themselves. Years of great trial and endurance have taught them to bear calamity without complaint. But I know that even small sums of money, promptly expended in the purchase of provisions for the poor among the sufferers, will greatly mitigate the immediate effects of this fearful calamity. The object of this letter is to suggest how contributions made here can be immediately applied to the relief of these people. Let such organizations as the Mercantile Exchanges, Board of Trade, Gold and Stock Exchange, &c., designate some one or more of your leading banking houses as a depository of funds contributed. I have no doubt some of them would cheerfully consent to receive and transmit the funds. Let all such deposits be made to the credit of Gilbert C. Walker, Governor of Virginia, whose large and generous heart and high position would insure the prompt and proper application of the charity. The Legislature has just met at Richmond. Governor Walker can organize committees of members from the devastated counties, who would at once through their boards of supervisors in the counties be able to distribute the finds properly in the purchase and delivery of flour, meal and salt to the destitute in their midst. I have had no time to correspond with Governor Walker on this subject, but I know the man and know how well and how energetically and faithfully he will perform this office of charity and philanthropy to a suffering people. If I can be of any service in bringing into communication parties who take hold of this matter here and Governor Walker or others in Virginia during my stay this well, I will cheerfully render it in behalf of the women and children of my suffering State, so suddenly cast down again from that hope and cheerfulness inspired by good crops and brighter prospects than they had enjoyed for ten years. I will be found daily at the office of the Virginia International Land, Loan and Trust company, 90 Broadway, over the National Bank of the Republic, from 10 till 2.
J.D. Imboden

TRANSCRIBED ARTICLE NO. 2

Mr. Wiltse's Letter: "To the Charitable,"
From the Norfolk Virginian, *October 26, 1870*

The following letter from one of the sufferers by the late flood was received by the Rev. M.J. Langhorne, of this city, a day or two since. A notice of the writer appeared in the news columns of our paper on Saturday, and we are assured by Mr. Langhorne, who has known him long and intimately, that all the statements which have been made are strictly true. Although Mr. Wiltse does not ask aid, he is in very destitute circumstances, and those of our citizens who may wish to help him in a pecuniary manner, can leave their donations with Mr. Langhorne, by whom they will be forwarded to the sufferer. We publish his letter in full:

Dear Brother Langhorne; - I have been wanting to write you for sometime, but I was not certain of your whereabouts. Doubtless you have seen in the papers that my family were drowned in the recent flood. Oh! was it not heart rending for me to see my dear wife and little ones perish in my sight, and no mortal hand could save them. If I had not asked, and obtained divine help, I would now have been a lunatic. My oldest was at school, he is the only one I have left out of five; I lost two some time ago, one of them drowned, and two in the recent flood, boy and girl. They might have come out, I was not at my house, but she did not apprehend any danger until it was too late. The water rose so fast we did not have time to do anything hardly we wanted to do. My house was near the river and was the first one surrounded, but it was not the first that went away. I was living at Rio Mills, on the Rivanna, six miles north of Charlottesville. The papers report Mr. Jennings and his wife drowned, but that is a mistake; he lost two children—one of their bodies has not been found yet. I recovered mine two days after, and they were nicely buried, all in one coffin. The little children lay in their mother's arms. Oh ! she was an affectionate wife and mother, and it was so hard for me to give her up. I was left in a very destitute condition; never recovered anything at all; have never seen a piece of my house, that I know of; it was broken to atoms. The people are very kind to me, and have given me clothing, and a little money, but I have not been able to get to business yet.

Let your petitions go up in my behalf, and write to me soon.

TRANSCRIBED ARTICLE NO. 3

An Appeal for Relief from the Virginia Legislative Relief Committee

"The Late Flood—An Appeal for Relief." From the *Norfolk Virginian*, October 26, 1870:

To the people of Virginia,

While the streams were still swollen with the waters of the flood which so recently devastated the larger portion of the State, the General Assembly received a message from the Governor informing them that several donations of money had been placed in his hands to be appropriated to the relief of the sufferers, and suggesting the propriety of taking some action to further the ends of charity to our fellow citizens.

The undersigned were then appointed a committee to consider what measures might be devised in the premises. They had scarcely assumed their duties when the hearts of the people, already sore and bleeding from their recent afflictions, were stricken with overwhelming anguish by the announcement of the death of General Lee. While the corpse of her best beloved son lay cold upon her bosom, the State could not bethink her for the time of the bereavements of her children, and all other tasks were laid aside, all other griefs forgotten, that we might commune and mourn together in our common sorrow, and do honor to our illustrious dead.

But now that we have laid our great citizen to his final rest, we cannot ignore our duty to the living; we must give ear to the pleading voices of distress which come to us from the regions which were ravaged by the devouring element. It needs no words to engrave forever upon the minds of those who witnessed it the terrible picture of wreck, and woe, and want that was presented in the track of the turbid waters. Throughout the wide and fertile section which lies between the Potomac and the James, and from the Alleghenies where the floods were gathered to the bay in which they precipitated their muddy currents laden with the spoils of wealth and industry, there was a scene of ruin which would have warmed the coldest heart to pity and wrestled aid from the hardest hand. All felt without suggestion the crying need for relief. We only asked ourselves what plan of general relief can we recommend for adoption. To the treasury of the State we could not turn. The want was so great and widespread, the State itself so poor, that the little she might have contributed would have crippled her still more than she is, and yielded but little benefit in the wide distribution. Without perplexing ourselves, then, to devise schemes which we could not execute, we resolved at once to turn to that resource to which the cry of feeble want has never, never been uttered in vain—we resolved to appeal to the people of Virginia themselves.

To you, then, people of Virginia, we bring our appeal to give what you can to relieve your unfortunate and needs brethren. Sharing, as you do, in the glory of that long succession of achievements which have made out State memorable and her sons honored among all nations of the Earth—sharing, too, in that series of misfortunes which have tried us with sterner tests and united us with even closer ties, shall we not turn with one accord from the sepulcher of our dead chief to exercise toward each those tender sympathies and enlarged charities of which he was so bright and beautiful an exemplar.

Long and dire as is the catalog of our calamities, this has been attended with more physical suffering than any that ever befell our State. War and conflagration never swept with a single blow so wide an arc never involved as once so many people; and the memory of the oldest inhabitant recalls no precedent to this sudden deluge. The high-water marks of other days were buried deep under the water, and history itself is at fault in searching the past for its equal. We must go back at least a century to find the memorials of a flood which can be named in comparison.

To those who reside upon or near the water courses which traverse the State from the mountains to the sea it were useless to recall the harrowing spectacle which met their eyes when the streams overleapt their accustomed channels, and swelling in volume with every pulse of the tide, deluged at once the growing crops and swept away the garnered fruits and the costly structures of years of culture and toil. Mills, locks, bridges, fences, barns, manufacturing establishments, were dashed to pieces or hurled away in the fury of the currents; and dwellings, with their inmates, were oftentimes caught up and lost together.

What adds with tenfold effect to the disastrous consequences of the flood was the unusual rapidity with which the streams arose, and the narrow region of the country to which the rains which preceded it were confined. In the more eastern portions of the State, there was little, if any rain. In the mountainous regions the very gates of Heaven seemed opened, and the torrents quickly accumulating rushed in heavy waves down the valleys into the lowlands, giving no warning of their coming until it was too late to escape them. This was a rare and exceptional case that a miller could remove his grain, a farmer his gathered crops, a manufacturer the implements or products of his manufactory, a storekeeping his merchandise or a family its household goods. Thus, in many cases, the family was cut off or surrounded before it was roused from its slumbers. Thus they were in many cases swept away with their fated homes, or had time only to fly naked or in dripping garments to find themselves houseless and homeless, stripped of all earthly possessions, and surrounded by friends unable to render them aid—whose want only embittered their own.

By the destruction of many of the largest industrial establishments that lined the streams, hundreds of laborers have been deprived of employment, and lost the only resource upon which they could rely for the support of their families. It cannot be hoped that a fund can be realized sufficient to fo more than relieve the actual and pressing wants of those placed in distressing circumstances, either by the immediate consequence of the flood to those incidents resulting. Five millions of dollars would not overreach the amount of losses in property, but a few thousand judiciously and promptly applied would go far to supply food, clothing and essential comforts to the more indigent and needy of the sufferers.

The committee have thought proper to address their appeal only to the people of Virginia, but they deem equally proper to say that any donations from the people of their sister States will be most gratefully received.

It affords them pleasure to record here the liberal contributions which have been forwarded to the Governor from citizens of other States. No sooner had the intelligence of the disaster been communicated to the country than latters or telegrams were received by him from the following parties, authorizing him to draw upon them for the respective amounts named:

John T. Underhill, Esq., President of the New York Stock Exchange, $2,000; Thomas A. Scott, Esq. Of Philadelphia, $1,000; T.P. Branch, Esq. Of Augusta, Ga, $50, Jacob G. Semon, Esq., Philadelphia, $50; Robert G. Loomis, Esq., Pittsburgh, Penn., $50; aggregating, $3,150.

These evidences of generous and active sympathy from abroad are peculiarly gratifying, and should stimulate those of our own people who have still the means to assist their fellows to energetic exertions and liberal donations.

[Missing line...]Co-operation of the citizens of the Commonwealth to secure its prompt and complete success.

Fellow citizens: It is for no sect or section, it is for no party or class, it is for no alien or distance or doubtful cause of charity, that we address you, but for your own kinsmen and countrymen, sprung from a common ancestry, nourished with you upon a common soil, who have shared with you a common history, who are bound to your common destiny, and who are at your doors throughout the Commonwealth in need of the necessities of life, we implore your aid.

Truly he gives twice who gives quickly to those who stand upon the verge of winter without food, shelter or clothing to protect them from its pinching wants.

W.D. Smith,
Charles Campbell,
Robert L. Owen,
Senate Committee.

A.M. Keiley,
S.S. Turner,
J.D. Jones,
P.Bradley,
J.W. Daniel,
House Committee.

PARTIALLY TRANSCRIBED LETTER FROM GENERAL JOHN D. IMBODEN TO HIS WIFE

From the Papers of John D. Imboden (1831–1895) 1937, Accession # 38-23, 580, 599, 2983, 2983-a, -b, Special Collections, University of Virginia Library, Charlottesville, Virginia.

Oct 9, 1870
(Partial transcription)

If you see the Richmond Whig you will see there a letter of mine from the NY Herald last week in regard to aid for our suffering people along the James & Shenandoah—In the engrossing cares of personal & public life here, my heart is in our dear old state, and the great distress of so many I feel calls upon me to do what I can to assist them. Ahead my letter has been the means of sending in some thousands of dollars to Gov. Walker to buy provisions. Dreadful as the Calamity has been it is a great relief to know that it has not reached your part of the state.

My own immediate family are considerable losers. My brothers are damaged not less than $2000 and my old father near 80 has had all his corn crop destroyed besides other losses—and many of my nearest friends have been nearly ruined. This wide spread and [?] distress has for over a week occupied so much of my thoughts that I have felt it was almost wicked to think only of my own individual happiness and had been doing ever since I parted from—And I have therefore spent several evenings in writing letters to others instead of to you, to give them such comfort as I can.

MINUTES OF THE NEW YORK STOCK EXCHANGE GOVERNING COMMITTEE

October 12, 1870 Transcription

October 12, 1870

A regular meeting of the Governing Committee was held this day in the Government Department room, at 2½ o'clock; 26 members present.
The President in the Chair.
The minutes of the last meeting, were read, approved.
A communication was received from the Stock Exchange with the request "that the sum of ___ Dollars, be appropriated, for the relief of the sufferers, by the recent flood in Virginia, half of said sum to be sent to the Governor of Virginia; and half to the Relief Committee Harper's Ferry; West Virginia."
W Hartshorne, briefly stated his reasons for opposing the applications; and concluded by offering the following
Whereas,

On the 26ᵗʰ January last, this Committee, "resolved that it was inexpedient to entertain any application for donations from any source, other than that of relief got members of the New York Stock Exchange." And
Whereas,

The condition of the finances of this Institution; and its contemplated expenditure do not warrant the Committee in departing from the rule then adopted—therefore
Resolved
That the Committee respectfully decline making the appropriation asked for.
Seconded and adopted.

RICHMOND MERCHANT LOSSES

As reported in the *Richmond Dispatch*, "Local Matters: The Flood Fallen—Losses by the Flood," October 4, 1870

BUSINESS/MERCHANT NAME	AMOUNT OF LOSS IN DOLLARS
A.A. Hutcheson	200
L. Harvey & Co.	500
J.E. Phillips & Co.	1,200
Moses Meyer	200
Farrar and Sherry	300
William Jenkins	300
Schaffer, Baker	200
Berrian & McPhall, druggists	450
O.A. Strecker, druggist	400
A. Bodeker, druggist	1,500
L. Powers, grocer	500 or 1,000
William S. Wood, tinner	500
H.M. Smith and Co., agricultural implements	2,000

Business/Merchant Name	Amount of Loss in Dollars
C. Zimmer, Confectioner	300
Geo. Guvernator, restaurant	300
A.G. Babcock, ice dealer	5,000
M. Kierstung, restaurant	200
D.D. Sullivan, grocer	300
W.A. Walsh & Co., grocers	300
W.H. Turpin, seedsman	300
Chas. T. Palmer, agricultural implements	2,500
R.H. Duke, grocer	500
Julius Kraker, clothing	1,800
B. Samuels, boots and shoes	200
S. Wallerstein, millinery	100
M. Golden, shoes &c.	200
Myer Kraker, dry goods	300
P. Weber, willow ware, etc.	1,600
H. Harris & Bro.	300
Moses Myer, clothing	200
Rose & Day, tin and stoves	400
L.T. Chandler	150
L. Oppenheimer	300
Jno. Allulai	250
J.E. L. Masurier	100
D. Baccagaluppi	350
Concani & Banachi	2,500
W.J. Harwood, shoes	100
Melti Larocca & Co., grocers	800
H.K. O'Dwyer, restaurant	300
M.J. Rosendorf, dry goods	500

Appendix E

Business/Merchant Name	Amount of Loss in Dollars
S.B. Lillenfield, dry goods and variety	3,000
J. Jacob, dry goods &c.	350
Joseph Strause	100
A.K. & H.C. Adams, grocers	100
Gresham & Sons, grocers	500
L. Lichtenstein	100
M. Golden, liquors	1000
James L. Porter, hardware	3,500
J.M. Higgins	150
S. Maccubbin, feed store	200
Cardwell & Co., agricultural implements	1,000
Ettenger & Edmond, machinists	1,500
Talbot & Sons, machinists	4,000
Mrs. Caroline Schwartz	200
G.S. Stacy & Son, mattress factory	200
C.F. Taylor, grocer	75
J.T. Vaughn, grocer	500
Herman Morris	400
M.J. Geradorf, machinist	400
S. Mason, grocer	50
B.C. Galloway	25
Smith & Potter, junk dealers	1,200
Currie & Co.	500
M. Lotterzo	200
W.H. Scott, druggist	1,200
B.G. Blythe	100
Adams & Co.	150
J.A. Lacy	200

BUSINESS/MERCHANT NAME	AMOUNT OF LOSS IN DOLLARS
J. Augustine	150
P. Levy & Sons	50
James River Steamboat Co. Sheds	2,000
J.R. Johnson & Co., Richmond steam forge & rolling mill	1,000
R.J. Smyth, ice dealer	1,600
Approximate Subtotal	54,100

NOTES

Introduction

1. "The Virginia Inundation," *New York Times*, October 3, 1870.
2. "Calamity at Harper's Ferry," *Wheeling Daily Register*, October 6, 1870.
3. Ibid.
4. Philena Carkin Papers, "Reminiscences of My Life and Work among the Freedmen of Charlottesville, Virginia, from March 1ˢᵗ 1866 to July 1ˢᵗ 1875." Philena Carkin Papers, 1866–1875, Accession #11123, Special Collections, University of Virginia Library, Charlottesville.
5. A freshet is a flood that results from precipitation, generally heavy rain or melted snow. The term has fallen out of favor in modern usage. However, it was widely used during the nineteenth century and will make several appearances in this work.
6. Chamber of Commerce Records, 1867–1985, Valentine Museum, Richmond, Virginia.
7. "The Late Destructive Flood," *Virginia Free Press*, October 8, 1870.

Chapter 1

8. "The Flood," *Rockingham Register*, October 13, 1870.
9. While there have been several other flooding events in Virginia, the 1870 flood is unusual because of the regional scale of death and destruction of property along several rivers. The 1877 flood was geographically similar, but there were few casualties and the water was not quite as high.

10. Reprinted from the *Lexington Gazette*, "The Flood," *Charlottesville Chronicle*, October 8, 1870.

11. "The Drought in Virginia," *Anderson Intelligencer*, September 22, 1870.

12. "Rain," *Charlottesville Chronicle*, September 28, 1870.

13. Wayland, *History of Shenandoah County*, 361.

14. "Lunch for Humorists," *Staunton Spectator*, September 27, 1870.

15. "Local Matters, The Freshet," *Charlottesville Chronicle*, October 1, 1870.

16. Papers of the John Horn Sawmill, Rockbridge Baths, Virginia, University of Virginia Special Collections.

17. Wayland, *History of Shenandoah County*, 361.

18. "Heavy Rain—Terrific Freshet," *Staunton Spectator*, October 4, 1870.

19. Ibid.

20. Ibid.

21. Ibid.

22. Ibid.

23. Ibid.

24. Ibid.

25. Ibid.

26. Ibid.

27. Letter from Ulysses S. Grant to Henry W. Halleck, July 14, 1864.

28. "The Late Flood," *Shenandoah Herald*, October 6, 1870.

29. I have located a few specific instances of bankruptcy and relocation. However, comprehensively enumerating the economic loss on an individual scale turned out to be outside of the scope of this book.

30. "Terrible Freshet—South River," *Staunton Spectator*, October 4, 1870.

31. Ibid.

32. 1870 U.S. Census, Augusta, Virginia, District 2, 14–15.

33. "Late Flood," *Richmond Dispatch*, October 8, 1870.

34 "Warm Springs Turnpike," *Rockingham Register*, October 13, 1870.

35. "North River in Rockingham," *Staunton Spectator*, October 4, 1870.

36. "The Great Flood—Special Telegram to the Dispatch," *Daily Dispatch*, October 5, 1870.

37. Ibid.

38. "The Great Flood, Disasters in Rockingham," *Daily Dispatch*, October 5, 1870.

39. "Terrible Freshet—South River," *Staunton Spectator*, October 4, 1870.

40. "Mount Vernon Iron Works," *Staunton Spectator*, October 25, 1870.

41. Ibid.

42. "Letter from the Shenandoah Valley," *Alexandria Gazette*, October 6, 1870.

43. *Staunton Spectator*, October 4, 1870.

44. "Flood," *Rockingham Register*, October 13, 1870.

45. Amanda Petefish, "Letter to Mary Sigler Downs," October 10, 1870. Original held at Port Republic Museum.
46. Ibid.
47. John F. Lewis, "The Flood in Rockingham," *Rockingham Register*, October 13, 1870.
48. Ibid.
49. Ibid.
50. Ibid.
51. Ibid.
52. Ibid.
53. Ibid.
54. Ibid.
55. Ibid.
56. Ibid.
57. Ibid.
58. Ibid.
59. Senator John Francis Lewis was elected to the U.S. Senate in January 1870, after Virginia's readmission to the Union. He also briefly served as lieutenant governor from October 1869 to January 1870. He was born in Rockingham County at Lynnwood Plantation, where he spent his life as an agriculturalist, when not involved in politics. He was elected as a Republican during all of his terms of public service. Prior to the Civil War, Lewis was a delegate to the 1861 Virginia Succession Convention, where he was the only member from east of the Allegheny Mountains who refused to endorse succession. As a testament to his popularity, Lewis served a second term as lieutenant governor from 1881 to 1886. He also served as a U.S. marshal for the western district of Virginia from 1875 to 1882.
60. Sometimes also called Riverbank.
61. "A Faithful Dog…," *Staunton Spectator*, October 25, 1870.
62. Ibid.
63. Ibid.
64. Ibid.
65. 1870 U.S. Census, Rockingham, Virginia, Stonewall Township, 33.
66. The *Staunton Spectator* reprinted the original version from the *Rockingham Register*. This story was also picked up by the *Alexandria Gazette*.
67. 1870 U.S. Census, Rockingham, Virginia, Stonewall Township, 33.
68. "The Great Flood," *Daily Dispatch*, October 5, 1870
69. Ibid.
70. 1870 U.S. Census, Rockingham, Virginia, Elk Run, 56.
71. "Flood," *Rockingham Register*, October 13, 1870.
72. Ibid.

73. Ibid.

74. Ibid.

75. Ibid.

76. Ibid.

77. 1880 U.S. Census, Virginia, Page County, Shenandoah Iron Works, 56.

78. "Flood," *Rockingham Register*, October 13, 1870

79. Ibid.

80. Mr. Stalling was likely G. Franz Stahling, who lived in Stephensburg. His profession was listed as "master painter" on the 1860 census; Shenandoah Centennial Association History Committee, *Shenandoah: A History of Our Town and Its People*, 9; "Flood," *Rockingham Register*, October 13, 1870.

81. "Flood," *Rockingham Register*, October 13, 1870.

82 "Vivid Picture of Flood Terrors," *Page News and Courier*, March 28, 1924.

83. B.W.P., "Correspondence of the Page Courier," *Rockingham Register*, December 22, 1870.

84. Ibid.

85. "Correspondence of the Page Courier," *Rockingham Register*, December 29, 1870.

86. Strickler, *Short History of Page County*, 228.

87. Virginia General Assembly, *Acts of the General Assembly*, 508; "New Registration," *Daily Dispatch*, October 19, 1870.

88. Virginia General Assembly, *Acts of the General Assembly*, 508.

89. "Interesting Correspondence," *Staunton Spectator*, September 13, 1870.

90. "The Shenandoah Iron Works," *Staunton Spectator*, September 27, 1870.

91. Shenandoah Centennial Association History Committee, *Shenandoah*, 9.

92. Age and death date were located through Find A Grave, www.findagrave.com.

93. Hotchkiss, *Shenandoah Iron, Lumber, Mining and Manufacturing*.

94. "Flood," *Rockingham Register*, October 13, 1870.

95. Ibid.

96. *Sketch of the Vicinity of the Shenandoah Iron Works on the South Fork of the Shenandoah River at Shenandoah Virginia*, www.loc.gov/resource/g3884s.cwh00247/

97. Wayland, *History of Shenandoah County*, 361.

98. Strickler, *Short History of Page County*, 217.

99. The ages and names of the Petty household are taken from the 1870 Census. Page County, Shenandoah Iron Works District, 8.

100. Strickler, *Short History of Page County*, 217.

101. Ibid.

102. Ibid.

103. Ibid., 218.

104. Ibid.
105. Ibid.
106. "More Freshet News," *Staunton Spectator*, October 18, 1870; Strickler, *Short History of Page County*, 218.
107. "More Freshet News," *Staunton Spectator*, October 18, 1870.
108. Strickler, *Short History of Page County*, 218.
109. Ibid.
110. Ibid.
111. Ibid.
112. Ibid.
113. Ibid., 219.
114. "A Richmond Man Drowned," *Rockingham Register*, October 12, 1870. Mr. West is also listed as a carpenter in the 1870 Boyd's City Directory. It is unclear why he was involved in purchasing southern bank notes. *Boyd's City Directory*, 234.
115. Wayland, *History of Shenandoah County*, 362.
116. William Martin, age twenty, is listed on the 1870 census as living and working with the Kite family. Page County Census, Shenandoah Iron Works District, 7.
117. Wayland, *History of Shenandoah County*, 362.
118. According to Thomas, *(Old) Farmer's Almanac*, 24, there was a new moon on September 25, 1870. The moon reached the first quarter on October 1.
119. Wayland, *History of Shenandoah County*, 362.
120. Ibid.
121. Ibid.
122. Ibid.
123. Ibid.
124. "More Freshet News," *Staunton Spectator*, October 18, 1870.
125. Ibid.
126. Wayland, *History of Shenandoah County*, 363.
127. Strickler, *Short History of Page County*, 219.
128. Ibid.
129. Ibid.
130. Ibid.
131. Ibid.
132. Ibid.
133. Ibid.
134. Ibid.
135. Ibid.
136. Ibid., 220.

137. Ibid.
138. Ibid., 221.
139. Page County Will Books, Volume L, p. 340-344.
140. Strickler, *Short History of Page County*, 221.
141. Ibid., 215–22.
142. "Richmond Man Drowned," *Rockingham Register*, October 13, 1870.
143. U.S. 1870 Census, Virginia, Henrico County, Marshall Ward, 21.
144. "History," White House Farm Foundation, https://www. whfarmfoundation.org/history; White House Farm National Register of Historic Places application https://www.dhr.virginia.gov.
145. "The Flood in the Page Valley," *Richmond Daily Dispatch*, October 7, 1870.
146. "More Freshet News," *Staunton Spectator*, October 18, 1870.
147. Ibid.
148. Strickler, *Short History of Page County*, 223.
149. "More Freshet News," *Staunton Spectator*, October 18, 1870.
150. Ibid.
151. Strickler, *Massanutten*, 78.
152. Strickler, *Short History of Page County*, 211.
153. Strickler, *Massanutten*, 79.
154. "Flood," *Rockingham Register*, October 13, 1870.
155. Carole Nash, personal communication, August 11, 2015; Major flooding events have followed and have, in turn, scoured and deposited almost another five inches of stratigraphic material over the past 145 years.
156. "The Flood," *Alexandria Gazette*, October 8, 1870
157. Ibid.
158. Mile estimates are taken from the Virginia Department of Game and Inland Fisheries, www.dgif.virginia.gov.
159. Wayland, *History of Shenandoah County*, 365–68.
160. Ibid., 366.
161. 1870 U.S. Census, Warren, Virginia, 1st Township, 50–51.
162. Wayland, *History of Shenandoah County*, 366.
163. Ibid.
164. Ibid.
165. Ibid.
166. Ibid.
167. Ibid., 368
168. Ibid.
169. Ibid., 366.
170. Ibid.

171. Ibid.
172. Ibid.
173. Ibid.
174. Ibid.
175. Ibid.
176. Ibid.
177. Ibid.
178. Ibid., 367.
179. Ibid., 366.
180. Ibid., 366–67.
181. Ibid., 367.
182. Ibid.
183. Ibid.
184. Ibid.
185. Ibid.
186. Ibid.
187. "The Late Flood," *Shenandoah Herald*, October 6, 1870
188. Ibid.
189. "Flood," *Alexandria Gazette*, October 8, 1870
190. "Late Flood," *Shenandoah Herald*, October 6, 1870.
191. Weston's Mill became known as Riverton Mills. The original mill was burned in the Civil War by General Sheridan. The burning is referenced in the Committee of War Claims Report to the 47th Congress. "John Torrey and Others" from the Committee on War Claims, 47th Congress, 1st Session, Report No. 1100, 3–4.
192. "Disastrous Freshets," *Shenandoah Herald*, October 6, 1870.
193. "Late Flood," *Shenandoah Herald*, October 6, 1870.
194. Ibid.
195. 1870 U.S. Census, Virginia, Shenandoah County, Ashby Township, 46.
196. "Missing," *Shenandoah Herald*, October 20, 1870.
197. "Supposed to be Drowned," *Shenandoah Herald*, October 6, 1870.
198. Find A Grave, www.findagrave.com/memorial/43758521/charles-d_-chamberlain.
199. "Late Flood," *Shenandoah Herald*, October 6, 1870.
200. Ibid.
201. Ibid.
202. Ibid.
203. Ibid.
204. "Late Destructive Flood," *Virginia Free Press*, October 8, 1870, 2.

Chapter 2

205. "Terrible Flood in Virginia," *Shepherdstown Register,* October 8, 1870.
206. "The Great Flood—The Flood in the Shenandoah Valley," *Alexandria Gazette,* October 3, 1870.
207. "Clarke County," *Spirit of Jefferson,* October 11, 1870.
208. "Terrible Flood in Virginia," *Shepherdstown Register,* October 8, 1870.
209. "The Flood in Clarke County," *Richmond Dispatch,* October 5, 1870.
210. "The Great Flood—Further News from the Lower Valley," *Daily Dispatch* (Richmond VA), October 6, 1870.
211. "Clarke County," *Spirit of Jefferson,* October 11, 1870; full name and age were located on the 1870 census. 1870 U.S. Census, Virginia, Clarke County, Greenway District, 29.
212. "Clarke County," *Spirit of Jefferson,* October 11, 1870.
213. Ibid.
214. Ibid.
215. Ibid.
216. "Great Flood—Further News from the Lower Valley," *Daily Dispatch* (Richmond VA), October 6, 1870.
217. "Flood in Clarke County," *Richmond Dispatch,* October 5, 1870.
218. "Late Flood," *Shenandoah Herald,* October 6, 1870.
219. "Terrible Flood in Virginia," *Spirit of Jefferson,* October 4, 1870.
220. "Lost," *Spirit of Jefferson,* October 29, 1870.
221. "Great Flood—Further News from the Lower Valley," *Daily Dispatch* (Richmond VA), October 6, 1870.
222. Ibid. Several newspapers printed this story with the incorrect name Daniel Altstadt. However, with further research, it was revealed that John married Annie Cockrell, John Griggs Cockrell's daughter. The Daniel Altstadt living in the area had passed away several years before the flood.
223. "The Great Flood—Further News from the Lower Valley," *Daily Dispatch* (Richmond VA), October 6, 1870.
224. "Deserved Public Mention," *Spirit of Jefferson,* October 18, 1870.
225. "Calamity at Harper's Ferry—Graphic Narrative of an Eyewitness," *Wheeling Daily Register,* October 6, 1870.
226. Ibid.
227. Ibid.
228. Ibid.
229. "Deserved Public Mention," *Spirit of Jefferson,* October 18, 1870.
230. Ibid.
231. Ibid; ages and names pulled from 1870 census records, specifically Jefferson County, Bolivar Township pages 17, 18, 49, 53.

232. "Deserved Public Mention," *Spirit of Jefferson*, October 18, 1870.

233. Ibid.

234. Ibid.

235. Ibid.

236. "Calamity at Harpers Ferry Graphic Narrative of an Eyewitness," *Wheeling Daily Register*, October 6, 1870.

237. "Terrible Flood in Virginia," *Spirit of Jefferson*, October 4, 1870.

238. "Late Destructive Flood," *Virginia Free Press*, October 8, 1870, 2.

239. "Calamity at Harpers Ferry Graphic Narrative of an Eyewitness," *Wheeling Daily Register*, October 6, 1870.

240. Professions taken from the 1870 census.

241. Surkamp, "Free, Black Families in Jefferson County."

242. Barry, *Strange Story of Harper's Ferry*, 191.

243. Ibid.

244. "Calamity at Harpers Ferry Graphic Narrative of an Eyewitness," *Wheeling Daily Register*, October 6, 1870.

245. "Sadly, Truly…" *Shepherdstown Register*, October 8, 1870.

246. Ibid.

247. Ibid.

248. "Calamity at Harpers Ferry Graphic Narrative of an Eyewitness," *Wheeling Daily Register*, October 6, 1870.

249. Ibid.

250. Ibid. Ages and professions taken from the 1870 U.S. Census, West Virginia, Jefferson County, Bolivar District, page 21 and 12.

251. "Calamity at Harpers Ferry Graphic Narrative of an Eyewitness," *Wheeling Daily Register*, October 6, 1870.

252. Ibid.

253. Ibid.

254. Ibid.

255. Ibid.

256. Barry, *Strange Story of Harper's Ferry*, 178–79.

257. "Calamity at Harpers Ferry Graphic Narrative of an Eyewitness," *Wheeling Daily Register*, October 6, 1870.

258. 1870 U.S. Census, West Virginia, Jefferson County, Bolivar District, 53.

259. Ibid.

260. Ibid.

261. "Calamity at Harpers Ferry Graphic Narrative of an Eyewitness," *Wheeling Daily Register*, October 6, 1870. Names and ages taken from a combination of the 1870 census, 1860 census and official death records.

262. 1860 U.S. Census, Virginia, Jefferson County.

263. "Calamity at Harpers Ferry Graphic Narrative of an Eyewitness," *Wheeling Daily Register*, October 6, 1870.

264. Ibid.

265. Barry, *Strange Story of Harper's Ferry*, 180–81.

266. "Calamity at Harper's Ferry—Graphic Narrative of an Eyewitness," *Wheeling Daily Register*, October 6, 1870.

267. Ibid.

268. Ibid.

269. Ibid.

270. Ibid.

271. Ibid.

272. Ibid.

273. Ibid.

274. "Terrible Flood in Virginia," *Spirit of Jefferson*, October 4, 1870.

275. Ibid.

276. "Calamity at Harpers Ferry Graphic Narrative of an Eyewitness," *Wheeling Daily Register*, October 6, 1870.

277. Borden, Archaeological Investigations, 2.

278. "Calamity at Harpers Ferry Graphic Narrative of an Eyewitness," *Wheeling Daily Register*, October 6, 1870.

279 Ibid.

280. Ibid.

281. "Terrible Flood in Virginia," *Spirit of Jefferson*, October 4, 1870.

282. "Calamity at Harpers Ferry Graphic Narrative of an Eyewitness," *Wheeling Daily Register*, October 6, 1870.

283. Ibid.

284. Ibid.

285. Ibid.

286. Ibid.

287. Ibid.

288. Ibid.

289. Ibid.

290. Ibid.

291. Ibid.

292. "Late Destructive Flood," *Virginia Free Press*, October 8, 1870, 2.

293. "The Late Disastrous Flood," *Virginia Free Press*, October 8, 1870.

294. "Terrible Flood in Virginia," *Spirit of Jefferson*, October 4, 1870.

295. Ibid.

296. Ibid.

297. "Late Destructive Flood," *Virginia Free Press*, October 8, 1870, 2.

298. Ibid.

299. Ibid., 2.
300. Ibid.
301. "Late Disastrous Flood," *Virginia Free Press*, October 8, 1870.
302. "The Flood at Berlin," *Wheeling Daily Intelligencer*, October 5, 1870.
303. Ibid.
304. Ibid.
305. Ibid.
306. "Late Destructive Flood," *Virginia Free Press*, October 8, 1870, 2.
307. Ibid.
308. "Disastrous Freshets," *Shenandoah Herald*, October 6, 1870.
309. Ibid.
310. Ibid.
311. "Letter from Loudoun," *Alexandria Gazette*, October 5, 1870.
312. Ibid.
313. "Correspondent at the Great Falls," *Georgetown Courier*, October 8, 1870,
314. "Canal Navigation," *Alexandria Gazette*, October 11, 1870.
315. "The Flood in the Potomac," *Alexandria Gazette*, October 3, 1870.
316. "The Great Destruction of Property," *Evening Star*, October 3, 1870.
317. "Effects of the Great Storm," *Evening Star*, October 1, 1870.
318. Ibid.
319. "Livestock Swept Off," *Evening Star*, October 3, 1870.
320. Effects of the Great Storm," *Evening Star*, October 1, 1870.
321. Ibid.
322. Ibid.; "Boats Found," *Georgetown Courier*, October 14, 1870.
323. "Effects of the Great Storm," *Evening Star*, October 1, 1870.
324. Public Acts of the Forty-First Congress of the United States, 41st Congress, 3rd Session 1871, 428.
325. "A Child's Hand," *Evening Star*, October 3, 1870
326. "Effects of the Great Storm," *Evening Star*, October 1, 1870.
327. "Great Flood," *Evening Star*, October 3, 1870
328. Ibid.
329. Ibid.
330. "The Flood in the Potomac," *Alexandria Gazette*, October 3, 1870.
331. Ibid.
332. "The Freshet," *Evening Star*, October 4, 1870.
333. Ibid.
334. Ibid.
335. Ibid.
336. "The Flood Which Raged Here…" *Georgetown Courier*, October 8, 1870.
337. "Effects of the Great Storm," *Evening Star*, October 1, 1870.
338. "Wyman, the Wizard," *Evening Star*, September 29, 1870.

339. "Effects of the Great Storm," *Evening Star*, October 1, 1870.
340. Ibid.
341. Ibid.
342. Ibid.
343. Ibid.
344. "Jackson City Under Water," *Evening Star*, October 3, 1870.
345. Ibid.
346. "Adventures of a Haystack," *Evening Star*, October 3, 1870.
347. "The Great Flood," *Evening Star*, October 3, 1870.
348. "The Freshet," *Evening Star*, October 4, 1870.
349. Ibid.
350. "Great Flood," *Evening Star*, October 3, 1870
351. Since that bridge fell under federal jurisdiction, the repair required an act of Congress, appropriation of funds and approval by the chief of engineers of the army. Although Congress appropriated $100,000 in 1872, the final cost of repair was $91,000; "A Quartet of Bridges: Structures Across which a Million People Annually Pass," *Washington Post*, September 21, 1884.
352. "The Long Bridge Has Since…" *Georgetown Courier*, October 8, 1870.
353. Ibid.
354. "Quartet of Bridges," *Washington Post*, September 21, 1884.

Chapter 3

355 "Flood in the James," *Alexandria Gazette*, October 3, 1870.
356. "Great Flood," *Richmond Whig*, October 3, 1870.
357. "Rockbridge County," *Staunton Spectator*, October 11, 1870.
358. Papers of the John Horn Sawmill.
359. "Remarkable Rain," *Virginia Gazette*, September 30, 1870; "Letter from Lexington," *Daily Dispatch*, September 30, 1870.
360. "Remarkable Rain," *Virginia Gazette*, September 30, 1870.
361. "Rockbridge County," *Staunton Spectator*, October 11, 1870.
362. "Letter from Lexington," *Daily Dispatch*, October 7, 1870.
363. Ibid.
364. "Rockbridge County," *Staunton Spectator*, October 11, 1870.
365. Ibid.
366. Ibid.
367. Ibid.
368. "Letter from Lexington," *Daily Dispatch*, October 7, 1870.
369. Ibid.

370. Ibid.
371. Ibid.
372. Ibid.
373. Ibid.
374. Ibid.
375. Ibid.
376. Ibid.
377. Ibid.
378. Ibid.
379. William Nalle, letterm October 16, 1870, Manuscript #0042, Virginia Military Academy.
380. "Proof about Coffin for General Lee," 422.
381. "Funeral of General R.E. Lee," 188.
382. "Proof about Coffin for General Lee," 422.
383. "Funeral of General R.E. Lee," 188.
384. "Rockbridge County," *Staunton Spectator*, October 11, 1870.
385. Ibid.
386. "Above Lynchburg," *Richmond Whig*, October 5, 1870.
387. "Rockbridge County," *Staunton Spectator*, October 11, 1870
388. U.S. Department of Commerce, *Fourteenth Census of the United States, State Compendium, Virginia*, 8.
389. "Great Freshet at Lynchburg," *Richmond Dispatch*, September 30, 1870.
390. Ibid.
391. Ibid.
392. "From Lynchburg. Graphic Account of the Devastation by Flood and Fire," *Daily Dispatch* (Richmond, VA), October 4, 1870.
393. "Great Freshet at Lynchburg," *Richmond Dispatch*, September 30, 1870.
394. "From Lynchburg. Graphic Account of the Devastation by Flood and Fire," *Daily Dispatch* (Richmond, VA), October 4, 1870.
395. "Great Freshet at Lynchburg," *Richmond Dispatch*, September 30, 1870.
396. "From Lynchburg. Graphic Account of the Devastation by Flood and Fire," *Daily Dispatch* (Richmond, VA), October 4, 1870.
397. "Great Freshet at Lynchburg," *Richmond Dispatch*, September 30, 1870.
398. Ibid.
399. "From Lynchburg. Graphic Account of the Devastation by Flood and Fire," *Daily Dispatch* (Richmond, VA), October 4, 1870.
400. Ibid.
401. Ibid.
402. "Great Freshet at Lynchburg," *Richmond Dispatch*, September 30, 1870.
403. "Sandy Hook—Loss of Life," *Richmond Whig*, October 1870.
404. This particular incident was difficult to unravel because there are so

many conflicting accounts with missing information about who was on the bridge embankment. The constant is always Mrs. Ransom, her daughter and domestic servant (Martha was never mentioned by name), along with several children of Mr. Whitlow. Sometimes an African American woman and her daughter and a Booker Johnson are included. For the book, an account from the *Lynchburg News* was chosen. Since Robert Whitlow is mentioned by name in other accounts and he is listed on the census as a household near other people who were named, it is likely his children were on the bridge. The author found his eldest son, Cary, and wife, Elizabeth, through Find A Grave and confirmed that they were not victims. It's likely that his thirteen-year-old son, Willie, died, as he is mentioned by name in a few accounts, but none of the other children is ever referred to.

405. "The Freshet Thursday Night," *Lynchburg News*, October 1, 1870.

406. Ibid.

407. "The Freshet Thursday Night," *Lynchburg News*, October 1, 1870.

408. 1870 U.S. Census, Virginia, Campbell County, Eastern Division, 50.

409. Ibid.

410. Ibid.

411. "Terrible Flood in the James River," *Lynchburg News*, September 30, 1870.

412. Ibid.

413. "From Lynchburg. Graphic Account of the Devastation by Flood and Fire," *Daily Dispatch* (Richmond, VA), October 4, 1870.

414. "Terrible Flood in the James River," *Lynchburg News*, September 30, 1870.

415. Ibid.

416. Ibid.

417. Ibid.

418. "From Lynchburg. Graphic Account of the Devastation by Flood and Fire," *Daily Dispatch* (Richmond, VA), October 4, 1870; "Freshet Thursday Night," *Lynchburg News*, October 1, 1870.

419. "From Lynchburg. Graphic Account of the Devastation by Flood and Fire," *Daily Dispatch* (Richmond, VA), October 4, 1870.

420. Ibid.

421. Ibid.

422. Ibid.

423. Ibid.

424. Ibid.

425. Ibid.

426. "Post-Diluvian Further Particulars of the Flood," *Richmond Whig*, October 4, 1870.

427. "From Lynchburg. Graphic Account of the Devastation by Flood and Fire," *Daily Dispatch*, October 4, 1870.

428. Ibid.
429. Ibid.
430. "Post-Diluvian Further Particulars of the Flood," *Richmond Whig*, October 4, 1870.
431. "Freshet Thursday Night," *Lynchburg News*, October 1, 1870.
432. Ibid.
433. Ibid.
434. Ibid.
435. Ibid.
436. "Particulars of the Flood at Lynchburg," *Daily Dispatch* (Richmond, VA), October 3, 1870.
437. "The Great Flood: Letter from Nelson County," *Richmond Whig*, October 11, 1870.
438. Ibid.
439. Ibid.
440. Ibid.
441 1870 U.S. Census, Virginia, Nelson County, Lovingston, 107.
442. Ibid., 49.
443. "Great Flood: Letter from Nelson County," *Richmond Whig*, October 11, 1870.
444. Lorraine, *Guide to the Works of the James River*, 12.
445. "Great Flood: Letter from Nelson County," *Richmond Whig*, October 11, 1870.
446. Ibid.
447. Ibid.
448. *Charlottesville Chronicle*, October 8, 1870.
449. "Great Flood: Letter from Nelson County," *Richmond Whig*, October 11, 1870.
450. "Further Loss of Life by the Flood," *Richmond Whig* October 6, 1870. Reprinted from the *Lynchburg Republican*, October 5, 1870, and also in the *Richmond Daily Dispatch*, October 6, 1870.
451. Ibid.
452. The author searched through 186 Woodsons on the Virginia 1870 census. None of them held the occupation of "boatman."
453. "Great Flood: Letter from Nelson County," *Richmond Whig*, October 11, 1870.
454. Ibid.
455. "Further Loss of Life by the Flood," *Richmond Whig*, October 6, 1870.
456. 1870 U.S. Census, Virginia, Nelson County, Lovingston, 105
457. "Further Loss of Life by the Flood," *Richmond Whig*, October 6, 1870.
458. Ibid.

459. James Jones, born June 22, 1868.
460. "Great Flood: Letter from Nelson County," *Richmond Whig*, October 11, 1870.
461. Ibid.
462. "Letter," October 30, 1870, Papers of William Daniel Cabell and the Cabell and Ellet families, UVA Special Collections.
463. Ibid.
464. "Storm and Flood," *Alexandria Gazette*, September 30, 1870.
465. Ibid.
466. Ibid.
467. Ibid.
468. Ibid.
469. "Terrible Flood in Virginia," *Spirit of Jefferson*, October 4,1870.
470. "The Bridge at Waynesboro," *Richmond Daily Dispatch*, October 1, 1870.
471. "The Freshet," *Charlottesville Chronicle*, October 1, 1870.
472. J.L.B. "The Freshet—Five Lives Lost," *Charlottesville Chronicle*, October 8, 1870.
473. Ibid.
474. Ibid.
475. "The Scottsville Register," *Charlottesville Chronicle*, October 8, 1870.
476. "The Scottsville Register," *Rockingham Register*, December 8, 1870.
477. 1870 U.S. Census, Fluvanna County, Virginia, population schedule, taken June 13, 1870, 1. Wyatt is listed as "mulatto" on the census, but is referred to as "colored" in the newspaper.
478. Commissioner of Claims, "Claim for Joseph Wyatt, No. 22117, Albemarle County, Virginia," submitted May 25, 1874. Deposition page 5. National Archives and Records Administration.
479. 1870 U.S. Census, Virginia, Albemarle County, St. Anne Parrish, 36.
480. "Freshet—Five Lives Lost," *Charlottesville Chronicle*, October 8, 1870.
481. 1870 U.S. Census, Albemarle County, Virginia, population schedule, taken July 12, 1870, 32.
482. "Correspondence of the Whig." *Richmond Whig*, October 5, 1870.
483. Ibid.
484. Richard L. Nicholas, "War Comes to Scottsville," *Scottsville Museum Newsletter* no. 24, 4–8, https://scottsvillemuseum.com/war/1865WarInScottsville/WarComesToScottsville.pdf.
485 Commissioner of Claims, "Claim for Joseph Wyatt, No. 22117, Albemarle County, Virginia" Submitted to Congress December 5, 1877.
486. "Local Matters, The Freshet," *Charlottesville Chronicle*, October 1, 1870.
487. Ibid.

488. Ibid.; The Jennings family had 7 children according to the 1870 census. It's likely that the two lost in the flood were Robert (five) and Angelina (three). 1870 U.S. Census, Virginia, Albemarle County, Fredericksville, 197.

489. "To the Charitable," *Norfolk Virginian*, October 26, 1870.

490. See appendix C, page 159, for transcribed letter.

491. "To the Charitable," *Norfolk Virginian*, October 26, 1870.

492. "A Sad Case," *Rockingham Register*, October 27, 1870.

493. Ibid.

494. "To the Charitable," *Norfolk Virginian*, October 26, 1870.

495. Strickler, *Short History of Page County*, 221.

496. "From the Charlottesville Chronicle, 4th Instant," *Lynchburg Daily News*, October 6, 1870.

497. "Insanity of Mr. Ransom," *Petersburg Daily Courier*, October 5, 1870. Reprinted from the *Lynchburg Virginian*.

498. Ibid.

499. Ibid.

500. "The Body of Mrs. Ransom," *Lynchburg Daily News*, October 13, 1870; "Body Identified," *Lynchburg Daily News*, October 19, 1870; "Identification of a Drowned Woman," *Lynchburg Daily News*, October 21, 1870.

501. "To the Charitable," *Norfolk Virginian*, October 26, 1870

502. Philena Carkin Papers, "Reminiscences of My Life and Work," 117–18.

503. Ibid.

504. Ibid.

505. Ibid.

506. Ibid., 119–20

507. Ibid

508. Ibid.

509. Ibid.

510. Ibid., 123–24.

511. Ibid.

512. Ibid.

513. Ibid.

514. Ibid.

515. Ibid.

516. Ibid.

517. Ibid.

518. The terms *southern* and *conservative* are separated in this sentence because the story also ran in a conservative paper from an area that would traditionally be considered northern.

519. "A Sad Incident," *Baltimore Sun*, October 6, 1870.

520. Ibid.

521. It may have also been printed in other locations; however, these are the ones that were able to be located using optical character recognition software and the American Memory newspaper database.
522. "A Characteristic Incident," *Charleston Daily News*, October 14, 1870; "A Characteristic Incident," *Anderson Intelligencer*, October 20, 1870; "A Characteristic Incident," *Fairfield Herald* (Winnsboro, SC), October 26, 1870.
523. "Characteristic Incident," *Charleston Daily News*, October 14, 1870.
524. Hodgson and Wakeham, "Hodgson & Wakeham," Library of Virginia, Broadside Collection.
525. Fluvanna Civil War Commission, *Fluvanna County Sketchbook 1777–1963*, Whittet & Shepperson, Richmond, Virginia, 1963, 39.
526. "Great Flood," *Richmond Whig*, October 3, 1870.
527. Ibid.
528. "The Rise of the James," *Daily Dispatch*, October 3, 1870.
529. "The Tobacco Injured at Mayo's Warehouse," *Richmond Whig*, October 3, 1870; "The Flood in the James," *Alexandria Gazette*, October 3, 1870.
530. Alison Holcomb, "Analyzing an Artifact: What in the World Is a Hogshead?" NCpedia, ncpedia.org/tobacco/barrels.
531. "Flood in the James," *Alexandria Gazette*, October 3, 1870.
532. "Great Flood," *Richmond Whig*, October 3, 1870.
533. "Rise of the James," *Daily Dispatch*, October 3, 1870.
534. Ibid.
535. Ibid.
536. Ibid.
537. Ibid.
538. Ibid.
539. Ibid.
540. Ibid.
541. Ibid.
542. Ibid.
543. Ibid.
544. Ibid.
545. Ibid.
546. Ibid.
547. Ibid.
548. Ibid,
549. "Great Flood," *Richmond Whig*, October 3, 1870.
550. Ibid.
551. "Flood in the James," *Alexandria Gazette*, October 3, 1870.
552. "After the Flood," *Richmond Whig*, October 4, 1870.
553. "Flood in the James," *Alexandria Gazette*, October 3, 1870.

554. "Great Flood," *Richmond Whig*, October 3, 1870.
555. Ibid.
556. "Flood in the James," *Alexandria Gazette*, October 3, 1870.
557. Ibid.
558. Even though it was a known site that flooded several times after the 1870 flood, Main Street Station was built on the site of the St. Charles Hotel in 1901. It was heavily damaged by Hurricane Agnes almost one hundred years later in 1972.
559. "Great Flood," *Richmond Whig*, October 3, 1870.
560. Hargrove, "Richmond [blank] 185 [blank]," Library of Virginia, Broadside Collection.
561. "Great Flood," *Richmond Whig*, October 3, 1870.

Chapter 4

562. "To the Charitable," *Norfolk Virginian*, October 26, 1870.
563. According to an inflation calculator this should be about $3,072.06 in 2019 U.S. dollars. This property is listed in the 1870 Albemarle census records.
564. The events of this paragraph are taken from a letter written by Wiltse that was published in the *Norfolk Virginian* on October 26, 1870. The information about his occupation and personal property wealth is from the 1870 census. A full transcription of the letter can be found in appendix C.
565. There is a fair amount of research devoted to the Johnstown Flood, the Chicago Fire and the Peshtigo Fire. However, these events receive the majority of scholarship for nineteenth-century American disasters. The author chose not to examine the Johnstown Flood for comparison because it took place nineteen years after the 1870 flood and had a unique set of circumstances that shaped the relief efforts.
566. John D. Imboden, "The Late Flood," *New York Herald*, October 4, 1870.
567. "Appeal," *Virginia Free Press*, October 8, 1870.
568. John D. Imboden, "The Late Flood," *Richmond Whig*, October 6, 1870.
569. Ibid
570. Papers of John D. Imboden.
571. Tripp, *Yankee Town, Southern City*, 32.
572. Governor Gilbert C. Walker, Executive Papers.
573. Younger and Moore, *Governors of Virginia*, 59.
574. Ibid., 60.
575. Ibid., 61.
576. In October 1870, Walker appears to be in the good graces of the state legislature and the general public. He was working to promote his debt

plan, and at this point, it was still being debated. In 1871, things would take a turn when the Readjuster movement started to rise.

577. General John D. Imboden "Letter to Gov. Walker" October 8, 1870. *Executive Papers of Governor Gilbert Carleton Walker, 1869–1873*, Library of Virginia.

578. "The Virginia Disaster," *Sweetwater Enterprise*, October 6, 1870.

579. "In a Few Days Our Citizens Will Doubtless Be Called…" *Philadelphia Inquirer*, October 4, 1870.

580. "The Great Flood," *New York Times*, October 5, 1870.

581. Ibid.

582. Data compiled from multiple letters and telegraphs found in the *Executive Papers of Governor Gilbert Carleton Walker, 1869–1873*, Library of Virginia.

583. "Governor's Message," *Lynchburg Daily News*, October 10, 1870; "General Assembly of Virginia," *Lynchburg Daily News*, October 10, 1870.

584. "Flood Relief Fund," *Norfolk Virginian*, October 20, 1870.

585. Sawislak, *Smoldering City*, 81.

586. Sharpe, *In the Shadow of the Dam*, 98.

587. Ibid., 121–22.

588. The twenty-day figure is based on the published relief letter from the Legislative Flood Relief Committee that explained the delay in fundraising efforts. See appendix C for transcribed letter.

589. "Help Them," *Lynchburg Daily News*, September 30, 1870.

590. "An Appeal for Aid," *Lynchburg Daily News*, October 3, 1870.

591. Ibid.

592. Tripp, *Yankee Town, Southern City*, 59.

593. Ibid., 61–62. African Baptist was created as a separate congregation under the umbrella of supervision by First Baptist as a mission church. During the early 1850s, African Baptist was briefly granted autonomy to manage its own affairs, but the congregation reverted to the jurisdiction of First Baptist when there was a concern about its autonomy.

594. "Thanks," *Lynchburg Daily News*, October 8, 1870.

595. "Help Them," *Lynchburg Daily News*, September 30, 1870

596. "An Appeal for the Relief of Suffering Humanity," *Lynchburg Daily News*, October 3, 1870.

597. "A Shame," *Lynchburg Daily News*, October 6, 1870.

598. "All Persons Having Money…" *Lynchburg Daily News*, October 5, 1870.

599. "Meeting of the Ministers of Lynchburg—Relief of the Sufferers by the Flood," *Lynchburg Daily News*, October 19, 1870; "Baptist Church" does not have an additional signifier in the article.

600. Tripp, *Yankee Town, Southern City*, 181.

601. Ibid.

602. Ibid

603. Ibid

604. Ibid.

605. "Flood Relief Fund," *Norfolk Virginian*, October 20, 1870.

606. Tripp, *Yankee Town, Southern City*, 194.

607. Ibid.

608. Ibid., 211.

609. Ibid., 204.

610. Chicago Relief and Aid Society, *Chicago Relief.*

611. The official reported number is actually wrong. After viewing the donation letters Governor Walker saved, this number should be $3,600. The inaccuracy comes from attributing only $50 to T.P. Branch, who was the first donor and generously gave $500, not $50. Unfortunately, this is not a simple typo in a singular newspaper but actually found in the committee's official letter to the public and aggregated as "$3150." This could be a simple oversight but more likely seems indicative of the carelessness of the committee. To be incorrect when reporting five donations seems to be a glaring error. By the governor's own papers, the committee raised a total of $4,569.27, only about $1,000 more after it released the final appeal for aid. In 2019 dollars, this equates to approximately $93,580.54.

612. Chicago Relief and Aid Society, *Chicago Relief*, 13.

613. Sawislak, *Smoldering City*, 119.

614. Chicago Relief and Aid Society, *Chicago Relief*, 17.

615. Total amount was compiled from Governor Walker's executive papers.

616. "Vivid Picture of Flood Terrors," *Page News and Courier*, March 28, 1924.

617. The author's estimate includes the nine families mentioned by name, along with the addition of at least five houses in the town of Shenandoah, Slabtown and the sixteen families who received relief in Springfield. This is also including the attribution of one African American woman's trip down the Shenandoah River in her cabin. Several articles mention that she was from Page County, but they are inconclusive, since her name was never disclosed.

618. "Letter to Page Courier," *Page Courier*, December 2, 1870.

619. This information was found by comparing the names on the distribution list to the 1870 census records for this area.

620. 1870 U.S. Census, Springfield Township, Page County, Virginia, 41.

621. John W. Watson, "Editor Courier—Sir I Send You…" *Page Courier*, December 16, 1870; Washington J. Jackson was the secretary of the Commercial Exchange, Philadelphia.

622. "The Good Old City," *Rockingham Register*, October 15, 1870. Reprinted from the *Warren Sentinel.*

623. "Meeting of the Corn Exchange," *Alexandria Gazette*, October 22, 1870.

624. Ibid.

625. Ibid.

626. Ibid.

627. Ibid.

628. "The Corn Exchange Committee," *Alexandria Gazette*, October 22, 1870.

629. 1870 U.S. Census, Springfield Township, Page County, Virginia, Population Schedule, taken July 5, 1870, 44. Peter Glenn was likely the son of Emma Bixler Glenn and Mark Glenn, who were married on February 6, 1855, in Page County.

630. "Distribution by the Relief Committee," *Page Courier*, December 16, 1870.

631. Ibid.

632. "Meeting of the Corn Exchange," *Alexandria Gazette*, October 22, 1870.

633. "Letter to Page Courier," *Page Courier*, December 2, 1870.

634. "Distribution by the Relief Committee," *Page Courier*, December 16, 1870.

635. "An Appeal for Aid," *Norfolk Virginian*, October 26, 1870.

636. "Norfolk Mourns Departed Hero," *Norfolk Virginian*, October 14, 1870.

637. "Death of Gen. Lee," *Alexandria Gazette*, October 14, 1870.

638. "Letter from Lexington," *Richmond Daily Dispatch*, October 20, 1870.

639. "New York Subscriptions to the Virginia Sufferers," *Baltimore Sun*, October 10, 1870.

640. New York Stock Exchange, *Minutes of the New York Stock Exchange*, October 7–18, 1870. See appendix D.

641. *Governor Gilbert C. Walker, Executive Papers, 1869–1873*.

642. "Starting the Ball," *Rockingham Register*, October 13, 1870.

643. "Local Matters. Relief of Sufferers by the Flood…" *Daily Dispatch*, November 28, 1870.

644. Ibid.

645. Technically, this region of West Virginia was still under litigation to determine if it could legally separate from Virginia. The case was under review at the Supreme Court, but a final decision was not handed down until 1871.

646. "Relief for the Sufferers," *Virginia Free Press*, October 15, 1870.

647 "Frederick City, Maryland," *Spirit of Jefferson*, November 1, 1870.

648. "Ladies Relief Meeting," *Virginia Free Press*, October 29, 1870.

649 "Public Meeting," *Virginia Free Press*, December 24, 1870.

650. Ibid.

651. "The Disaster at Harper's Ferry—What Has Become of the Relief Fund?" *Baltimore American*, January 16, 1871.

652. Ibid. Kitemiller is likely a misspelling of Kitzmiller. There was an Archibald M. Kitzmiller who was the chief clerk to the superintendent of the armory at Harpers Ferry in 1860.

653. "Harper's Ferry," *Shepherdstown Register,* January 28, 1871.

654. Ibid.

655. "Harper's Ferry Relief Committee," *Virginia Free Press*, April 15, 1871.

656. Sharpe, *In the Shadow of the Dam*, 121.

657. Ibid., 122.

658. Sawislak, *Smoldering City*, 85.

659. Ibid., 71.

660. Ibid.

661. The president of the counter-committee, John W. Neer, was a local businessman in Harper's Ferry who had a stake in the relief efforts. According to local historian Robert H. Moore II, Neer lost his $3,000 lumber business in the flood and was unable to financially recover. He would eventually declare bankruptcy and have to leave the city. For more information, "Did People Call Him a Union Man?" "Yes sir, and a great many called him a damn Yankee all the time." http://cenantua. wordpress.com/2012/07/07/did-people-call-him-a-union-man-yes-sir-and-a-great-many-called-him-a-damn-yankee-all-the-time.

662. Manchester is now a part of the City of Richmond. However, in 1870, it was still a part of Chesterfield County. It is directly across the James River on the other side of Mayo's Bridge. Although it would not likely have qualified for city-sponsored aid, if there was a local committee, they would have likely benefited.

663. "More Losses Reported," *Richmond Whig*, October 4, 1870.

664. "Local Matters, The Rise of the James…" *Richmond Dispatch*, October 3, 1870.

665. "Local Matters, The Flood Fallen…Losses by the Flood," *Richmond Dispatch*, October 4, 1870. See appendix C.

666. "After the Flood," *Richmond Whig*, October 4, 1870.

667. Ibid.

668. "Miscellaneous," *Richmond Dispatch*, October 3, 1870.

669 "After the Flood," *Richmond Whig*, October 4, 1870.

670. He was called Landrum Nelson in the *New York Herald* and Landon Henderson in the *Richmond Whig*. Having not found individuals by either name, the author believes that the individual in question may have been Landrum Henderson, a corporal in Company 37, USCT, who lived in the Richmond area after the war.

671. "The Storm Still Raging at Richmond," *New York Herald*, October 3, 1870.

672. "After the Flood," *Richmond Whig*, October 4, 1870.

673. Ibid.

674. "A Benefit for the Sufferers of the Flood," *Richmond Dispatch*, October 3, 1870.

675. Katz, *Undeserving Poor*, 6.

676. Ibid., 2.

677. Ibid.

678. "After the Flood," *Richmond Whig*, October 4, 1870.

679. Ibid.

680. Common Council of the City of Richmond, *Charter and Ordinances*, 244.

681. "The Richmond Calamity," *Harper's Weekly*, May 14, 1870, 306.

682. Chamber of Commerce Records, 1867–1985. MS. C 58. Valentine Museum. Richmond, VA, Volume 2, 260.

683. The reporting for the casualties and those affected by the capitol disaster is worded as such: "The number of persons actually visited, all more of less injured, is 199; the number of beneficiaries, families or dependent connections of the injured, is 652; the number of widows aided is 31; the number of male survivors who are permanently injured is 17." The capitol disaster was responsible for the deaths of 60 people, while the flood was responsible for about 100. The flood rendered about 350 families homeless, while the capitol disaster caused financial hardship and potential destitution to 652 people. It us unknown how many individuals made up the 350 families, but the two events are somewhat comparable in scale.

684. It's unclear how much, if any, money was raised because those documents no longer exist. However, there were active calls for fundraising and planning that began around this time.

685. "The Damage by the Flood," *Richmond Whig*, October 7, 1870.

686. "The Remedy," *Richmond Whig*, October 4, 1870.

Chapter 5

687. "Stone Pillar, Turned Turtle, Undermines High Water Talk," *Richmond Dispatch*, April 1, 1936.

688. "A Disastrous Freshet," *Daily Dispatch*, November 26, 1877.

689. "Stone Pillar, Turned Turtle, Undermines High Water Talk," *Richmond Dispatch*, April 1, 1936.

690. "Flood Marker of 1771," National Register of Historic Places Nomination Form, 1970, 2.

691. Vaughn, *Luray and Page County Revisited*, 105.

692. "Shaft to Kite Family Erected," *Daily News Record*, September 3, 1938.

693. "The Dedication and Unveiling…" *Daily News Record*, June 16, 1938.

694. Ibid.

695. The spring of 1937 saw a boost in production and wages, and the unemployment rate dipped to 14.3 percent for the year. The jump to a 19 percent unemployment rate in 1938 may have influenced travel in 1938. According to the *Page News and Courier*, there was a 6.7 percent drop in visitors to the Shenandoah National Park in July 1938 (versus July 1937). "Shenandoah National Park Continues to Show Small Drop in Patronage," *Page News and Courier*, September 2, 1938; unemployment statistics from http://www.u-s-history.com/pages/h1528.html.

696. The floods that are recorded as being higher in this area are the 1771 flood (estimated to be 40.0–45.0 feet), Hurricane Juan in 1985 (31.8 feet) and Hurricane Agnes in 1972 (34.02).

697. Scottsville Museum, "Scottsville Floods," http://scottsvillemuseum.com/floods/home.html.

698. Canal Basin Square, museum plaque, Scottsville, Virginia. Visited June 20, 2014.

699. Scottsville Museum, "Scottsville Floods," http://scottsvillemuseum.com/floods/home.html.

700. "Late Destructive Flood," *Virginia Free Press*, October 8, 1870, 2.

Appendix B

701. "Distribution by the Relief Committee," *Page Courier*, December 16, 1870.

BIBLIOGRAPHY

Archives and Manuscript Collections

The Library of Virginia, Richmond, Virginia

Hargrove, James B. "Richmond [blank] 185 [blank]: Dear Sir, I Beg
  Leave to Inform You I Have Taken the Auction Room under the St.
  Charles Hotel…for the Selling of Slaves…" Library of Virginia, Special
  Collections, Broadside Collection.
Hodgson, Geo P., Jas. O. Wakeham. "Hodgson & Wakeham, successors to
  Hodgson & Son, General Store." Columbia, Virginia, Library of Virginia,
  Special Collections, Broadside Collection.
Walker, Governor Gilbert C. Executive Papers, 1869–1873, Accession
  40233. State Government Records Collection, The Library of Virginia,
  Richmond, Virginia.

Port Republic Museum, Port Republic, Virginia

Petefish, Amanda. "Letter to Mary Sigler Downs." October 10, 1870.
  Original held at Port Republic Museum.

University of Virginia, Special Collections, Charlottesville, Virginia

Brown Family Papers and Store Ledgers, 1811–1875, Accession 4117,
  Special Collections Department, University of Virginia Library,
  Charlottesville, Virginia.

John Horn Saw Mill Papers, 1852–1876, Accession #11289, Special Collections Department, University of Virginia Library, Charlottesville, Virginia.

Milbourne, Virginia Strickler. Page County Virginia Papers, Accession #4148, Special Collections Department, University of Virginia Library. Charlottesville, Virginia.

Papers of John D. Imboden (1831–1895) 1937, Accession # 38-23, 580, 599, 2983, 2983-a, -b, Special Collections, University of Virginia Library, Charlottesville, Virginia.

Papers of William Daniel Cabell and the Cabell and Ellet families, Accession #276, 276-a, 283, 1154, 1210, 1744, Special Collections, University of Virginia Library, Charlottesville, Virginia.

Philena Carkin Papers, 1866–1875, Accession #11123, Special Collections Department, University of Virginia Library, Charlottesville, Virginia.

Walker Family Correspondence, 1853–1936, Accession #5042, University of Virginia Library, Charlottesville, Virginia.

The Valentine Museum, Richmond, Virginia

Richmond Chamber of Commerce. Chamber of Commerce Records, 1867–1985, MS. C58, Valentine Museum, Richmond, Virginia.

Richmond History Vertical File: James River—Floods, Valentine Museum, Richmond, Virginia, 132.

Virginia Museum of History and Culture, Richmond, Virginia

C.R. Rees & Company. Photographic print, Richmond Flood, 1870 19th C. Accession No. 2000.132, Virginia Historical Society.

PUBLISHED GOVERNMENT DOCUMENTS

Common Council of the City of Richmond. *The Charter and Ordinances of the City of Richmond*. Richmond, VA: V.L. Fore, Printer, 1869.

United States Army Signal Corps. *Annual Report of the Chief Signal Officer Made to the Secretary of War for the Fiscal Year Ended June 30, 1871*. Washington, D.C.: Government Printing Office, 1871.

United States Census Office. Population schedules of the ninth census of the United States, 1870. Virginia, Albemarle County. Washington, D.C.: National Archives and Records Service, General Services Administration, 1965.

———. Population schedules of the ninth census of the United States, 1870. Virginia, Fluvanna County. Washington, D.C.: National Archives and Records Service, General Services Administration, 1965.

———. Population schedules of the ninth census of the United States, 1870. Virginia, Page County. Washington, D.C.: National Archives and Records Service, General Services Administration, 1965.

United States House of Representatives. "John Torrey and Others" from the Committee on War Claims, 47th Congress, 1st Session. Report No. 1100., p. 3–4, in *Index to the Reports of the Committees of the House of Representatives for the First Session of the Forty-Seventh Congress 1881–82*, in 6 vols. Vol. 4. Washington, D.C.: Government Printing Office, 1882.

Virginia General Assembly. *Acts and Joint Resolutions passed by the General Assembly of the State of Virginia, at Its Session of 1870–'71*. Richmond, VA: C.A. Schaffter, Sup't of Public Printing, 1871.

———. *Acts of the General Assembly of the State of Virginia*. Richmond, VA: J.E. Goode, 1870.

Other Primary Sources

Boyd's Directory Company. *Boyd's Directory of Richmond City and a Business Directory of Norfolk, Lynchburg, Petersburg, and Richmond, Together with a Compendium of the Government, Courts, Institutions and Trades*. Richmond, VA: Bates & Waddy Brothers. 1870.

Chicago Relief and Aid Society. *Chicago Relief: First Special Report of the Chicago Relief and Aid Society*. Chicago: Culver, Page, Hoyne & Co., 1871.

Frank Leslie's Illustrated Newspaper. "The Great Flood at Richmond." October 22, 1870.

Grant, Ulysses S. Letter from Ulysses S. Grant to Henry W. Halleck, July 14, 1864.Transcription from the Encyclopedia of Virginia. www.encyclopediavirginia.org.

Harper's Weekly. "The Flood in Virginia." October 22, 1870.

Hill Directory Company. *Richmond City Directory, Containing a General Directory of the Citizens of Richmond and Manchester, and also a Business Directory of the Cities of Richmond, Petersburg, Norfolk, Portsmouth, Danville, Farmville, Lynchburg, Lexington, Staunton, Harrisonburg, Fredericksburg, Alexandria, and Charlottesville, etc., etc*. Richmond, VA: B.W. Gillis, 1871.

Hotchkiss, Jedediah. *The Shenandoah Iron, Lumber, Mining and Manufacturing Company of Virginia: A Report on Its Charter, Lands, Iron Ores and Other Minerals, Timber, Water-Powers, Ironworks and Other Improvements and Commercial Facilities, and the Advantages, Present and Prospective, Offered by It for the Cheap Manufacture of Iron and Steel in All Their Forms, the Mining and Shipping of Iron Ores, the Manufacture of Articles Made Chiefly from Wood, Iron and Steel.* Staunton, VA: Spectator Steam-Print. House, 1878.

Nalle, William. William Nalle Letter, Manuscript #0042 Archives, Virginia Military Academy.

New York Stock Exchange. Minutes of the New York Stock Exchange. October 7–18, 1870.

NEWSPAPERS

Abingdon Virginian (Abingdon, VA)
Alexandria Gazette and Virginia Advertiser (Alexandria, VA)
Anderson Intelligencer (Anderson Court House, SC)
Baltimore American and Commercial Advertiser (Baltimore, MD)
Baltimore Sun (Baltimore, MD)
Charlottesville Chronicle (Charlottesville, VA)
Clarke Courier (Berryville, VA)
Daily Courier (Petersburg, VA)
Frank Leslie's Illustrated Newspaper (New York, NY)
Harper's Weekly (New York, NY)
Lexington Gazette (Lexington, VA)
Lynchburg Daily News (Lynchburg, VA)
New York Herald (New York, NY)
New York Times (New York, NY)
Norfolk Virginian (Norfolk, VA)
Page Courier (Luray, VA)
Richmond Daily Whig (Richmond, VA)
Richmond Dispatch (Richmond, VA)
Rockingham Register (Harrisonburg, VA)
Salem Ledger (Salem, VA)
Shenandoah Herald (Woodstock, VA)
Shenandoah Valley (New Market, VA)
Shepherdstown Register (Shepherdstown, WV)
Spirit of Jefferson (Charlestown, WV)
Staunton Spectator (Staunton, VA)
Valley Register (Middletown, MD)
Virginia Free Press (Charlestown, WV)
Virginia Gazette (Lexington, VA)
Washington Evening Star (Washington DC)
Weekly Arizona Miner (Prescott, AZ)
Wheeling Intelligencer (Wheeling, WV)

SECONDARY SOURCES

Barry, Joseph. *The Strange Story of Harper's Ferry with Legends of the Surrounding Country.* Martinsburg, WV: Thompson Brothers, 1903.

Barton, Clara. *The Red Cross: A History of this Remarkable International Movement in the Interest of Humanity.* Washington, D.C.: American National Red Cross, 1898.

Blanton, Dennis. "The Great Flood of 1771: An Explanation of Natural Causes and Social Effects." In *Historical Climatic Variability and Impacts in the United States,* edited by C.J. Mock and L. Dupigny-Giroux, 3–21. Netherlands: Springer, 2009.

Borden, Anna C. "Archaeological Investigations of Lewis Wernwag's Sawmill, 46JF229, Virginius Island Harpers Ferry, West Virginia." Harpers Ferry, West Virginia, August 1995.

Canal Committee, Historic Richmond Foundation. *Richmond's Historic Waterfront: Rockett's Landing to Tredegar 1607–1865.* Richmond, VA: The Foundation, 1989.

Christian, W. Asbury. *Lynchburg and Its People.* Lynchburg, VA: J.P. Bell Company, 1900.

Dabney, Virginius. *Richmond: The Story of a City.* Revised and expanded. Charlottesville: University of Virginia Press, 1990.

Dauber, Michele Landis. *The Sympathetic State: Disaster Relief and the Origins of the American Welfare State.* Chicago: University of Chicago Press, 2013.

Federal Emergency Management Agency. *The Federal Emergency Management Agency: Publication 1.* Washington D.C.: U.S. Department of Homeland Security, FEMA, 2010.

Fluvanna Civil War Commission. *Fluvanna County Sketchbook 1777–1963.* Richmond, VA: Whittet & Shepperson, 1963.

Friedman, Morgan. The Inflation Calculator. www.westegg.com/inflation.

"Funeral of General R.E. Lee." *Southern Historical Society Papers* 41 (1915): 188–91.

Johnson, Willis Fletcher. *History of the Johnstown Flood.* Philadelphia, PA: Edgewood Publishing Company, 1889.

Katz, Michael B. *The Undeserving Poor: America's Enduring Confrontation with Poverty: Fully Updated and Revised.* New York: Oxford University Press, 2013.

Kelly, Relda T. "Clara Barton with the American Red Cross at the Johnstown Flood." Thesis, Lewis University Graduate School of Nursing, Romeoville, Illinois, 1989.

Lorraine, Charles Kemper. *A Guide to the Works of the James River & Kanawha Company from the City of Richmond to the Ohio River.* Virginia Canals and Navigations Society, 1986.

Lutz, Francis Earle. *A Richmond Album; A Pictorial Chronicle of an Historic City's Outstanding Events and Places*. Richmond, VA: Garrett & Massie, 1937.

McCullough, David. *The Johnstown Flood: The Incredible Story Behind One of the Most Devastating Disasters America Has Ever Known*. New York: Simon & Schuster Paperbacks, 1968.

Moore, Virginia. *Scottsville on the James: An Informal History*. Charlottesville, VA: Jarman Press, 1969.

"Proof about Coffin for General Lee," *Confederate Veteran* 18 (1910): 422.

Sawislak, Karen. *Smoldering City: Chicagoans and the Great Fire, 1871–1874*. Chicago: Chicago University Press. 1995.

Sharpe, Elizabeth M. *In the Shadow of the Dam: The Aftermath of the Mill River Flood of 1874*. New York: Free Press, 2004.

Shenandoah Centennial Association History Committee. *Shenandoah: A History of Our Town and Its People*, 1985.

Slap, Andrew L., "The Strong Arm of the Military Power of the United States: Chicago Fire, the Constitution, and Reconstruction." *Civil War History* 47, no. 2 (June 2001).

Strickler, Harry M. *Massanutten: Settled by the Pennsylvania, Pilgrim 1726*. N.p.: 1924.

———. *A Short History of Page County, Virginia*. Harrisonburg, VA: C.J. Carrier Company, 1996.

Surkamp, Jim. "Free, Black Families in Jefferson County, Va. Towns." Civil War Scholars. June 15, 2011. http://civilwarscholars.com.

Thomas, Robert B. *The (Old) Farmer's Almanac*. Boston: Brewer and Tileston, 1870.

Tripp, Steven. *Yankee Town, Southern City: Race and Class Relations in Civil War Lynchburg*. New York: New York University Press. 1999.

Vaughn, Dan. *Luray and Page County Revisited*. Charleston, SC: Arcadia Publishing. 2008.

Wayland, John W. *A History of Rockingham County, Virginia*. Harrisonburg, VA: C.J. Carrier Company, 1972.

———. *A History of Shenandoah County, Virginia*. Strasburg, VA: Shenandoah Publishing House, 1927.

Younger, Edward, et al. *The Governors of Virginia 1860–1978*. Charlottesville: University Press of Virginia, 1982

INDEX

ABOUT THE AUTHOR

Paula Green is a public historian with a master's degree in public history from James Madison University. Her undergraduate work and training as an anthropologist and archaeologist inform part of this work. In addition to her cross-discipline training, Paula has worked in the JMU Libraries for over twelve years as an interlibrary loan borrowing specialist. Her daily work includes quests to find obscure research material for her patrons. This is her first book.

Visit us at
www.historypress.com

CPSIA information can be obtained
at www.ICGtesting.com
Printed in the USA
BVHW061119070920
588230BV00013B/468